Accounting for Beginners

A Simple and Updated Guide to Learning Basic Accounting Concepts and Principles Quickly and Easily, Including Financial Statements and Adjusting Entries for Small Businesses

Warren Piper Ruell

© Copyright 2019 - All rights reserved.

The content contained within this book may not be reproduced, duplicated or transmitted without direct written permission from the author or the publisher.

Under no circumstances will any blame or legal responsibility be held against the publisher, or author, for any damages, reparation, or monetary loss due to the information contained within this book, either directly or indirectly.

Legal Notice:

This book is copyright protected. It is only for personal use. You cannot amend, distribute, sell, use, quote or paraphrase any part, or the content within this book, without the consent of the author or publisher.

Disclaimer Notice:

Please note the information contained within this document is for educational and entertainment purposes only. All effort has been executed to present accurate, up to date, reliable, complete information. No warranties of any kind are declared or implied. Readers acknowledge that the author is not engaging in the rendering of legal, financial, medical or professional advice. The content within this book has been derived from various sources. Please consult a licensed professional before attempting any techniques outlined in this book.

By reading this document, the reader agrees that under no circumstances is the author responsible for any losses, direct or indirect, that are incurred as a result of the use of information contained within this document, including, but not limited to, errors, omissions, or inaccuracies.

Description

This book provides an essential overview of the established principles and practices of the accounting profession.

The accounting profession is among the oldest of the world's occupations. Modern versions of accounting practices that represent global standards date back to medieval Europe and even earlier. The current age of rapid technological innovation and the seemingly endless news stories of financial scandals have brought the field of professional accounting to the forefront of the American conversation. Also, far from limiting opportunities in the field of professional accounting, technological advances and developments in global business and finance have made professional careers in accounting more relevant, more exciting, and more in-demand than ever.

Accounting for Beginners is written for the small business owner, the aspiring accountant professional, and the busy professional looking for a quick and handy reference of the major conventions that govern this exciting field. When you read *Accounting for Beginners* you will learn about accounting fundamentals, including:

- Definitions of accounting and how accounting differs from bookkeeping.
- Financial statements:

- The balance sheet
- The income statement
- The cash flow statement

· Double-entry accounting, including debits, credits, and how to record transactions in journals and ledgers.

· Cash accounting vs. accrual accounting.

Accounting for Beginners also covers some of the more technical aspects of accounting, such as:

· Depreciation of fixed assets.

· Amortization of intangible assets.

· Budgeting for operational activities and capital expenditures .

· Recording costs for inventory and Cost of Goods Sold.

Next, *Accounting for Beginners* discusses many of the important professional practice conventions and regulatory foundations that professional CPAs must understand before earning a license, including:

· Generally Accepted Accounting Principles (GAAP)

· Background information about regulatory agencies such as the SEC, the AICPA, the FASB, and the GASB.

· Differences between U.S. accounting standards and international standards.

Finally, *Accounting for Beginners* discusses some of the more pressing concerns that face many of today's most successful accounting professionals, such as:

- Important principles and conventions of professional accounting firms.
- Fraud and ethics.
- Current fields actively seeking qualified accountants.

Whether you are currently considering a major course of study, pondering a career change, or actively engaged as a mid-career professional, *Accounting for Beginners* will give you a thorough and comprehensive review of established practices, a detailed guide to many of the most fundamental account recording techniques, and an experienced critique of the most pressing concerns and challenges facing contemporary CPAs.

Table Of Contents

TABLE OF CONTENTS   7

INTRODUCTION   10

CHAPTER 1: ACCOUNTING FUNDAMENTALS AND FINANCIAL STATEMENTS   13

WHAT IS ACCOUNTING?   16
WHAT ARE FINANCIAL STATEMENTS?   22

CHAPTER 2: THE BALANCE SHEET   29

ASSETS   32
LIABILITIES   36
OWNER'S (STOCKHOLDERS') EQUITY   39
UNDERSTANDING THE BALANCE SHEET   42

CHAPTER 3: THE INCOME STATEMENT   45

BASICS OF THE INCOME STATEMENT   47
COMPONENTS OF AN INCOME STATEMENT   50
FORMAT OF AN INCOME STATEMENT   56
UNDERSTANDING THE INCOME STATEMENT   60

CHAPTER 4: THE CASH FLOW STATEMENT   69

WHAT IS A CASH FLOW STATEMENT?   71

ADJUSTING DATA FOR THE CASH FLOW STATEMENT	74
ADJUSTMENT METHODS	77
COMPONENTS OF THE CASH FLOW STATEMENT	79
SAMPLE CASH FLOW STATEMENT	85

CHAPTER 5: GENERALLY ACCEPTED ACCOUNTING PRINCIPLES   87

WHAT ARE GENERALLY ACCEPTED ACCOUNTING PRINCIPLES (GAAP)?	90
WHO ARE THE SEC, THE AICPA, THE FASB AND THE GASB?	92

CHAPTER 6: DOUBLE-ENTRY ACCOUNTING   99

DEBITS AND CREDITS	102
THE GENERAL JOURNAL	106
THE GENERAL LEDGER	110
THE TRIAL BALANCE	119

CHAPTER 7: CASH ACCOUNTING VS. ACCRUAL ACCOUNTING   126

THE CASH METHOD	128
THE ACCRUAL METHOD	129
EXAMPLES OF CASH VS. ACCRUAL ACCOUNTING	131

CHAPTER 8: DEPRECIATION OF FIXED ASSETS   137

STRAIGHT-LINE DEPRECIATION	138
ACCUMULATED DEPRECIATION	141
SALVAGE VALUE	144
GAIN OR LOSS ON SALE	145

CHAPTER 9: AMORTIZATION OF INTANGIBLE ASSETS   147

WHAT ARE INTANGIBLE ASSETS?	148
STRAIGHT-LINE AMORTIZATION	151

CHAPTER 10: INVENTORY AND COST OF GOODS SOLD (COGS)   156

INVENTORY	157
CALCULATING COST OF GOODS SOLD	163
CHAPTER 11: BUDGETING FOR YOUR BUSINESS	**167**
WHAT IS BUDGETING?	170
CHAPTER 12: IMPORTANT PRINCIPLES AND CONVENTIONS OF ACCOUNTING	**182**
LEARNING TO CLASSIFY DIFFERENT ACCOUNTS	184
CHAPTER 13: FRAUD AND ETHICS	**190**
FRAUD: DEFINITION AND CAUSES	193
CHAPTER 14: JOBS IN ACCOUNTING	**199**
CHAPTER 15: GLOSSARY	**202**
COMMON TERMS USED IN BOOKKEEPING AND ACCOUNTING	202
RESOURCES	**210**

Introduction

Accounting for Beginners: A Simple and Updated Guide to Learning Basic Accounting Concepts and Principles Quickly and Easily, Including Financial Statements and Adjusting Entries for Small Businesses provides and overview of essential concepts and practices for the accounting professional. *Accounting for Beginners* is the companion volume to *Bookkeeping for Beginners: Learning the Essential Basics of Bookkeeping for Small Businesses with Simple and Effective Methods Step-by-Step (Including Comprehensive Accounting, Financial Statements, and QuickBooks).*

Accounting and bookkeeping are related practices. As a result, both books discuss some of the same practices. However, there are important and fundamental differences between the responsibilities and concerns of the professional accountant and those of the professional bookkeeper. Chapter 1 discusses these differences in greater detail, but suffice it to say that although accounting addresses concerns that require more education, training and a higher level of authority, the focus of the accountant in many respects is much narrower than that of the bookkeeper. Whereas *Bookkeeping for Beginners* addresses some of the concerns of the accountant as they relate to the practice of professional bookkeeping, *Accounting for Beginners* explores the responsibilities of the accountant in greater depth and detail. In addition to an expanded discussion of double-entry accounting, cash vs. accrual methods, and financial statements, *Accounting for Beginners* also explores many areas that were not covered in *Bookkeeping for Beginners*, such as:

- Depreciation and Amortization
- Budgeting
- Inventory
- Generally Accepted Accounting Principles
- Fraud and Ethics

We hope you find this book a useful and reliable resources for all your professional accounting needs. Please also refer to the companion volume, *Bookkeeping for Beginners,* for more comprehensive coverage of all the essential principles and practices used in professional bookkeeping and accounting.

Chapter 1: Accounting Fundamentals and Financial Statements

Figure 1: Free Image

Accounting is among the oldest of all the world's professions. The earliest known forms of accounting date back to ancient Mesopotamia and parallel early developments in writing, counting, and money. Double-entry and modern accounting date back to the early medieval period in the Middle East among Jewish communities located in Iraq and Iran. Although some credit the invention of double-entry accounting to the Goryeo dynasty, which reigned in Korea from 912 through 1392, most people attribute all contemporary accounting methods to an Italian friar by the name of Luca Pacioli. A contemporary of Leonardo DaVinci, Pacioli's publication, *Summa de arithmetica, geometria, proportioni et proportionalita*, contains one of the first published descriptions of the double-entry accounting system. His system is still the standard for all professional accounting everywhere in the world. Pacioli is known as the "Father of Accounting."

Accounting is a fundamental part of the machinery not only of business, but of all of human civilization. Historians use accounting records for researching and archiving purposes; governments use accounting to ensure accountability, and businesses use accounting to increase efficiency and profitability. The interdependence of accounting to all human endeavors necessarily results in a system that can be complex and challenging. Yet, at the same time, the purpose of accounting is to translate these complexities into understandable and useful bits of information. This chapter provides a provides a concrete definition of accounting, a comparison of accounting to bookkeeping, and an overview of the main products of the accounting profession: financial statements.

What is Accounting?

Accounting is the professional practice of measuring, processing, analyzing, understanding, and communicating financial data about business, corporations and other officially recognized legal entities that engage in business transactions. The purpose of accounting is to gain an understanding of the financial condition—including its profitability, net value, and potential for growth—and then communicating that information to a wide variety of interested parties. Furthermore, accounting uses established rules and practices to ensure that information is communicated using a universally accepted and understood language.

By assessing the value of a company's assets, its liabilities, the amount of money invested into it by its owners and other shareholders, an accountant can establish a dollar figure to answer the question, "How much is my business worth today?" By assessing the amount of money a company has earned over a given period of time and subtracting the amount of money the same company has spent during the same period of time, an accountant can determine not only whether a business is profitable, but how profitable. Finally, by assessing how a company generates revenue and how it uses those funds, an accountant can determine how well a company manages its resources and whether there is any potential for growth or sustained production.

These three aspects of a company's finances are summarized in their financial statements—the balance sheet, the income statement, and the cash flow statement. Producing financial statements is one of the primary responsibilities of the professional accountant. By analyzing these three aspects of a company's finances—its net worth, its profitability, and its liquidity—a skilled accountant can make many determinations about a company's strengths or weaknesses.

Well-documented financial statements, in turn, are the only acceptable way for a business to present a record of its activities to the public or to any other interested parties, such as financial regulators and potential investors. If a business wants to secure a loan for new developments, the bank will request its financial statements. If a business wants to secure funding by seeking out new investors, the investors will request financial statements. If a business is audited by a financial regulatory agency, the auditors will request financial statements.

It is true that to succeed, a business must be able to provide its core goods and services in a competitive environment. However, without a sound financial foundation, no business will be able to afford the resources and infrastructure necessary to continue to offer those goods and services in any environment, regardless of competition. Thus, accounting provides the necessary foundation and framework required for long-term success in any area of business.

How Is Accounting Different from Bookkeeping?

For the most part, bookkeeping and accounting are regarded as separate but related professions; however, in many regards, the responsibilities of the bookkeeper and the accountant overlap. If accounting is the professional practice of measuring, processing, analyzing, understanding and communicating financial data, bookkeeping is the professional practice of recording all of the daily business transactions of a business that provide the information accountants need to formulate that financial data.

Bookkeeping may be thought of as the starting point of the "accounting cycle." The accounting cycle officially has six steps:

1. Analyzing and recording transactions
2. Posting transactions to the ledger
3. Preparing a trial balance
4. Preparing adjusting entries
5. Preparing an adjusted trial balance
6. Preparing financial statements

Thus, before an accountant can begin the cycle of accounting during any given period of financial activity, the bookkeeper must present a record of all the business transactions for that period. Put differently, the bookkeeper's responsibilities begin and end at ensuring every transaction of a business is recorded in an official journal. Once the bookkeeper has accomplished this goal, the information is handed off to the accountant, who translates those transactions into financial statements that tell the story of the business's financial life.

Bookkeeping is itself an important and valuable profession. However, the bookkeeping profession requires far fewer certifications than the accounting profession. Although many bookkeepers may be certified as accountants, many do not have any official qualifications or degrees. Often, the contributions of a professional bookkeeper may be valued more by the wide array of on-the-job experience with bookkeeping and recording systems in different types of environment than for any formal training in finance. It is possible to gain certification as a bookkeeper, but it is not legally required.

On the other hand, accounting requires extensive education and certification. Most accountants are either Certified Public Accountants, Certified Management Accountants, or Certified Internal Auditors. As these titles imply, each of these positions require the accountant to pass a certification test. Becoming an accountant requires a bachelor's degree in accounting or other approved field of study. In addition, accountants may need to complete an additional year of certification. In the United States, requirements may vary from state to state, but all states require passage of the Uniform Certified Public Accountant Examination, which is administered by the American Institute of Certified Public Accountants.

What Are Financial Statements?

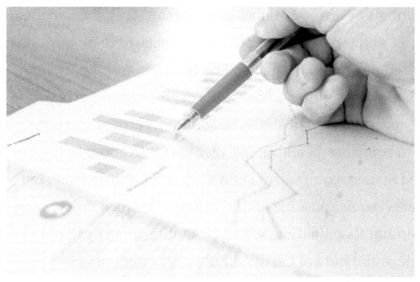

Figure 2: Free Image

As stated in the previous sections, the primary responsibility of the accountant is to produce financial statements that illustrate various aspects of a company's financial condition. The accounting profession has established three major reports that together comprise a company's official "financial statements." These statements are:

- Balance sheet
- Income statement
- Cash flow statement

Each of these statements focuses on a particular aspect of a company's financial picture. Specifically, the balance sheet illustrates how much a company is worth at a specific point in time, the income statement indicates how much money a company earned over a specified period of time, and the cash flow statement illustrates how the money earned revenue and whit is did with the money it earned.

To provide information that is specifically targeted and focused, each of the three financial statements must include certain types of information, while excluding certain other types of information. The following chapters provide greater detail, but we will provide a brief overview here.

The Basic Accounting Equation

To begin, all of accounting uses what is known as the "basic accounting equation." The basic accounting equation is:

$$Assets = Liabilities + Owner's\ Equity$$

As in any mathematical equation, the amounts on either side of the "equal sign" must be the same. For example, using simple math, all of the following equations are correct:

$$1+1+1+1=4$$
$$2+1+1=4$$
$$7-3=4$$
$$2+2=4$$

However, the following equations are incorrect:

$$1+5=4$$
$$2+2=5$$

The first of the three financial statements is the balance sheet, which shows a calculation of a company's net worth by showing the total value of its assets, the total value of its liabilities, and the total value of its owner's equity. Before the balance sheet can be distributed as an official statement of the company's net worth, the accountant must ensure that the data on the balance sheet conforms to the basic accounting equation, i.e., the total amount of the company's assets must be equal to the sum of its liabilities and owner's equity.

The income statement and the cash flow statement follow from the data included in the balance sheet. Thus, by ensuring first that the balance sheet conforms to the basic accounting equation, the accountant can be assured that the other two financial statements also contain accurate and reliable information.

Trial Balance

As stated earlier, there are six steps in the accounting cycle. The third step of this cycle is the preparation of what is known as a trial balance. The previous section illustrates how the basic accounting equation can help an accountant ensure that the information in a balance sheet is accurate and reliable. Of course, preparing financial statements—including the balance sheet—are the last step of the accounting cycle, so it stands to reason that the accounting cycle includes a mechanism for allowing the accountant to ensure that all the information recorded earlier by the bookkeeper is accurate and reliable. This procedure occurs in Step 3, when the accountant prepares trial balance.

The trial balance is an accounting worksheet that allows the accountant to verify the reliability of the data recorded by the bookkeeper. Although the trial balance is never released to shareholders with the three primary financial statements, it is an integral and indispensable component of the accounting cycle. The trial balance lists all of the accounts included in the general ledger (the accounts that are also listed in the chart of accounts). On the trial balance worksheet, the total closing balances of all the accounts are listed. In addition, these balances are listed as either debit balances or credit balances. So, for example, the closing balance of the cash account may have a debit balance of $2,500, while the closing balance of the accounts payable account may have a credit balance of $2,000.

Once the accountant has assembled all of the credit and debt balances for all the company's accounts at the closing of the financial period, he totals all the debits balances at the bottom the debt column and all the credit balances at the bottom of the credit column. As the equations required a company's assets to equal the sum of their liabilities and the owner's equities, a trial balance should result an equal figure for both debits and credits. If the total debit balances are not equal to the total credit balances, then the accountant must either locate errors in the bookkeeping records or enter adjusting entries to bring the books into balance before closing and producing financial statements.

Thus, throughout the professional system of bookkeeping and accounting, there are methods of checking for accuracy and reliability. Ultimately, when the accountant completes the entire accounting cycle, the resulting financial statements will provide the business owner with an accurate and concise picture of all the company's underlying financial activity for any given fiscal period.

Chapter 2: The Balance Sheet

XYZ Company
Balance Sheet
As at 30 June 2010

Current Assets		
Cash at bank	30,000	
Inventory	250,000	
Debtors	75,000	
Total current assets		355,000
Non - Current Assets		
Buildings	550,000	
Plant & equipment	250,000	
Vehicles	120,000	
Total non-current assets		920,000
Total Assets		**1,275,000**
Current Liabilities		
Credit cards	15,000	
Creditors	110,000	
Tax Payable	25,000	
Total current liabilities		150,000
Non-current Liabilities		
Long term loans		700,000
Total Liabilities		**850,000**
Owners Equity		
Capital	100,000	
Retained earnings	250,000	
Current earnings	75,000	
Total Owners Equity		**425,000**

Figure 3: Free Image

The balance sheet is one of the three main financial statements. (The other two are the income statement and the cash flow statement, both of which will be discussed in the next two chapters. In addition, some companies choose to also include a statement of stockholders' equity. You can read a definition of this fourth type of financial statements in the Glossary in Chapter 15). The balance sheet may also be referred to as a statement of financial position.

Generally, the purpose of a balance sheet is to present an overview of the issuing company's financial position by listing all of the company's assets, liabilities, and equity. The balance sheet possesses a characteristic that is fundamentally different form the income statement and the cash flow statement. Specifically, the balance sheet present financial information about a company that is relevant for a particular point in time only, whereas the income statement and the cash flow statement provide an overview of financial activity that covers a longer period of time—usually an entire year. Thus, because the balance sheet's strength illustrates the liquidity of a company—how much money and other assets they currently possess as opposed to how much money they owe—the balance sheet is often used when considering whether to issue a loan to a business. Of course, many other parties—including current and potential investors, management, suppliers, customers, competitors, and financial regulators—may also request a balance sheet to evaluate a company's current financial position. This chapter explores the three main components of the balance sheet, the many methods of financial analysis used to interpret balance sheet data, and how those analyses may be used by interested parties.

Assets

Remember that the basic accounting equation is **Assets = Liabilities + Owner's Equity**. This section discusses in detail what assets are and how the balance sheet allows accountants to provide information about a company's assets. In simplest terms, assets all of the property owned by a company that provides some type of value to the company, as expressed in dollars. There are many types and forms of assets. The most obvious example of an asset is cash. If your business uses a checking account to pay bills or for the deposit of money earned from the sale of goods and services, then the balance in the checking account is one of your primary assets. Your company may also have other types of cash accounts, such as a petty cash fund for per diem purchases. So-called "cash equivalent" accounts include short-term investments, such as certificates of deposit. Other financial assets include marketable securities, which are investments in stocks that can be sold for cash within one year.

Assets also include physical property, such as machinery and office furniture. Also referred to as fixed assets, these types of assets include all the major physical property, including office equipment, furniture, and machinery that your business needs to produce its core services. Fixed assets may include:

- Office furniture
- Office equipment

- Supplies
- Inventory
- Machinery
- Tools
- Land
- Land improvements
- Buildings

In addition to cash accounts and fixed assets, your balance sheet will also reflect the value of non-cash financial assets, such as prepaid expenses. These types of financial assets may include:

- Accounts receivable
- Prepaid rent or lease payments
- Prepaid insurance policies
- Prepaid legal fees or retainers
- Prepaid advertising
- Long-term investments (Securities such as stocks that will not be sold for cash.)

Finally, all of the assets listed above are generally classified as tangible assets—they are finite, physically identifiable assets. But assets may also include what are known as "intangible assets." Chapter 9 discuses intangible assets in detail, but we will mention them briefly here. Intangible assets are assets that are not physical—for example a patent, a copyright, an IP address, or a trademark. These assets can also add value to a company's net worth.

Generally, all asset accounts will have a debit balance. This may go against your natural way of thinking about debits. For example, if you use your debit card to make a purchase from your checking account, your balance declines and if you return the item to the store for a refund, your checking account will be credited for the amount of the purchase. However, the terms "debit" and "credit" are used differently in accounting, and depending on the type of account, a debit or a credit balance may indicate either a positive or negative balance. (Contra accounts are used in accounting to provide accountants with a way to offset potential gains or losses that fall outside the normal course of business. So, contra assets are asset accounts with credit balances that allow accountants to record discrepancies resulting from unpaid accounts receivable, deprecation, etc.)

Accountants follow a specific formula for showing a company's assets on the balance sheet. On a vertical balance sheet, assets are always listed at the top of the balance sheet. On a horizontal balance sheet, they are always listed on the left of the balance sheet. Regardless of whether the balance sheet uses a vertical or horizontal format, assets are listed in the following order:

- Current Assets
    - Cash and cash equivalents
    - Marketable securities
    - Accounts receivable
    - Inventory
    - Prepaid expenses
- Investments
- Fixed Assets (Property, Plant, and Equipment)
- Intangible Assets
- Other Assets

Liabilities

Whereas assets show all the property owned by a company, liabilities shows all of a company's outstanding financial obligations to creditors. Because liability accounts show amounts that must be paid, these accounts often have the word "payable" in the account title. Remember that a balance sheet is controlled by the basic accounting equation: Assets = Liabilities + Owner's Equity. Because we know that the assets are all the property that a company owns, we can think of liabilities as the unpaid portion for the cost of purchasing those assets. Put differently, liabilities are the source of a company's assets.

In addition to money owed, liabilities also include the "Unearned revenues" account. This account includes goods or services for which money has been received, but which have not yet been delivered. Because the company still retains the inventory and has not spent the manpower and resources to provide the goods or services that were sold, this type of income cannot yet be considered an asset, so it is placed in the Unearned Revenue account under Liabilities on the Balance Sheet.

Following are examples of the types of accounts that may be included under liabilities on a balance sheet:
- Accounts Payable
- Notes Payable

- Salaries Payable
- Interest Payable
- Other Accrued Expenses Payable
- Income Taxes Payable
- Customer Deposits
- Warranty Liability
- Lawsuits Payable
- Unearned Revenues
- Bonds Payable

These accounts will be further categorized according to whether they are current liabilities or long-term liabilities. Current liabilities are those liabilities that must be paid within one year from the date of the balance sheet; long-term liabilities are payable at a time beyond one year from the date of the balance sheet.

Liability accounts normally carry a credit balance. And as with asset accounts, contra liability accounts allow accountants to adjust for potential discrepancies resulting from uncertainties in the business environment. (For example, a lender may change the terms of repayment, resulting in a reduction in the amount owed by a company on a note or a bond.) Contra liability accounts normally carry a debit balance and may include accounts such as:

- Discounts on Notes or Bonds Payable
- Debt or Bond Issue Costs

As when reporting assets, accountant must also use standardized formats to report liabilities. On a vertical balance sheet, liabilities will appear under assets; on a horizontal balance sheet, liabilities will appear at the top of the left column. Regardless of whether the accountant uses a vertical or horizontal balance sheet, liabilities will be grouped under the following categories and shown in the following order:

- Current liabilities
    - Accounts payable
    - Accrued expenses
    - Notes payable
    - Wages payable
    - Interest payable
    - Taxes payable
    - Warranty liability
    - Unearned revenues
- Long-term liabilities
    - Notes payable
    - Bonds payable
    - Other long-term debt

Owner's (Stockholders') Equity

As with liabilities, the owner's (or stockholders') equity is also the source of a company's assets. Recalling again the basic accounting equation: Assets=Liabilities + Owner's Equity, the Owner's Equity portion of this equation is often referred to as the "book value" of a company because it reflects the remaining value when the amount that must be paid is subtracted from the value of what is already owned. The residual is the owner's equity in the company—the amount the company would be left with if all liquid assets were sold and converted to cash and all outstanding bills were paid. We can rewrite the basic accounting equation by solving for Owner's Equity to show this relationship:

Assets=Liabilities + Owner's Equity

(Assets) - **Liabilities**=(Liabilities + Owner's Equity) - **Liabilities**

Asset-Liabilities=Owner's Equity

On a balance sheet, the term "Owner's Equity" is used if the business is a sole proprietorship. However, if the company is a corporation—whether publicly traded or privately held—the term Stockholders' Equity is used to reflect the fact that the company is funded in part through the issuance of stocks; thus, there is more than one owner.

The types of accounts in this section of the balance sheet will be different depending on whether the company is a sole proprietorship or a corporation. In a sole proprietorship, owner's equity accounts may include:
- Capital
- Current Year's Net Income

Although the Stockholders' Equity section occupies the same position on the balance sheet and serves the same accounting purpose, the account types will be different than for a sole proprietorship. Types of corporate Stockholders' Equity accounts may include:
- Preferred Stock
- Common Stock
- Paid-in Capital in excess of par value
- Paid-in capital from treasury stock
- Retained Earnings
- Accumulated Other Comprehensive Income

Equity accounts normally have a credit balance, and like both asset and liability accounts, they may be offset by contra accounts to allow the accountant to make adjustments for uncertainties or discrepancies. Contra equity accounts normally carry a debit balance.

Owner's Equity accounts are usually limited in number, but an example of an Owner's Equity contra account may be:

- Drawing (the account from which the owner draws a salary)

Examples of contra accounts for Stockholders' Equity may include:
- Treasury Stock

On both vertical and horizontal balance sheets, the Owner's (Stockholders' Equity) appears just below the Liabilities section; on a horizontal balance sheet, this section will appear on the left side. Although there is no legally-mandated format to which all balance sheets must conform, accounting conventions require that this section of the balance sheet shows Equity accounts in a standardized format, with accounts in order and organized by category.

Generally, Owner's Equity accounts will be organized as follows:
- Capital
- Drawing
- Current Year's Net Income

For Stockholders' Equity, accounts will be organized by category, as follows:
- Paid-in Capital
- Retained Earnings
- Accumulated Other Comprehensive Income
- Treasury Stock

Understanding the Balance Sheet

The balance sheet is unique among the three main financial statements because it represents an aspect of a company's financial condition only for a specific point in time—the date the balance sheet was created. Both the Income Statement and the Cash Flow Statements (discussed in the next 2 chapters) show aspects of a company's financial condition over a period of time. Thus, this "snapshot" of a company's finances that a balance sheet provides is used differently by various financial analysts to gain an understanding of a company's underlying financial structure. Specifically, a balance sheet by itself cannot indicate whether the business is experiencing any trends that develop over a period of time, such as growth in certain areas or losses in certain underperforming sectors. As a result, these types of analyses using a balance sheet can only be made by comparing any given balance sheet with a balance sheet for the same company from a different time period, or with the balance sheets of other businesses in the same industry.

As stated earlier, the primary use of the balance sheet is to indicate the relationship among the three elements of the basic accounting equation. The balance sheet not only allows financial analysts to determine the value of assets owned by a company and the amount of money owed by a company, but also the company's net worth, or "book value."

Accountants can also use balance sheets to create various ratios that communicate information about a company's financial health to potential investors. One such ratio is the debt-to-equity ratio (D/E). The D/E is calculated by dividing the total liabilities by owner's (shareholders') equity. The D/E helps potential investors assess a company's ability to use financial leverage by showing how much of a company's operations are financed by debt as compared to cash or other wholly owned funds. The D/E also shows whether a company would be able to pay off all its debts in the event of total liquidation.

The Net Working Capital Ratio (NWC) represents the difference between a company's current assets and its current liabilities. This ratio measures several aspects of a company's liquidity, such as the efficiency of its operations and its ability to pay bills in the short-term. A company with a positive working capital ratio is more likely to attract investors; a company with a negative NWC may have more difficulty paying its creditors.

Another ratio derived from balance sheets is the acid-test ratio, which helps financial analysts determine whether a company's short-term assets are sufficient to pay for its short-term liabilities. Also called the quick ratio, the acid-test ratio is calculated using the following formula:

(Cash + Marketable Securities + Accounts Receivable)

$$\text{Acid Test} = \frac{}{\text{Current Liabilities}}$$

The resulting figure derived from dividing these specific assets by current liabilities produces a number greater than or less than 1. If a company's acid test is less than 1, it does not have enough liquid assets to pay its current liabilities. An acid test number that is significantly lower than the NWC indicates that the company's assets are comprised mostly of inventory. While this is generally not a good sign, some retail businesses whose revenue is derived mostly from selling inventory items may have a low acid test number that does not necessarily indicate financial instability.

Chapter 3: The Income Statement

Figure 4: Free Image

Like the balance sheet discussed in Chapter 2, the income statement is one of the three main financial statements. (The other is the cash flow statement, which will be discussed in the next chapter. In addition, some companies choose to also include a statement of stockholders' equity. You can read a definition of this fourth type of financial statements in the Glossary in Chapter 15). The income statement is also known as the statement of operations, the profit and loss statement, the statement of earnings, and the statement of revenue and expense. In many cases, a company may be required to submit an income statement to the Securities and Exchange Commission (SEC) or other financial regulators or financial institutes. In other cases, a company may simply produce an income statement for its own internal uses; these types of income statements are generally referred to as profit and loss statements.

Unlike the balance sheet, which provides a so-called "snapshot" of finances at the time the report is generated, income statements provide information about a company's financial performance over a specified period of time. Specifically, the income statement provides insight into the company's profitability by providing details about its revenues, its expenses, and its resulting profit (or loss). This chapter provides detailed information about the standard format of an income statement, some clarifications about how each section should highlight the company's performance, and some definitions about some of the key terms recorded in the income statement.

Basics of the Income Statement

Income statements are used to assess the profitability of a company over a specified period of time. The time period—which may be a week, three weeks, a month, five months, a year, or any other time interval—is always specified at the top of the income statement. To show a company's profitability, the income statement shows a company's revenues (the amount earned from all activity) and a company's expenses (the amount of money they had to spend to provide goods and services). Generally, the difference between revenues and expenses shows the company's net profit for the time period indicated at the top of the income statement. Although the basic concept of the income statement is easy to understand, a properly formatted income statement is more complicated and involves the use of many accounting principles.

Accrual vs Cash Accounting

First, all income statements must use the accrual method of accounting. The reason for this rule is that the purpose of the income statement is to provide insight into a company's profitability over time, not just the amount of cash it has received or spent at any specific point in time.

We'll use an example to illustrate the difference between cash accounting and accrual accounting. Let's say Smith Tech Repair offers computer maintenance services to all offices operating in the downtown area. In February, Mr. Smith, the owner of Smith Tech Repair, provided routine maintenance for desktop and laptop machines at 1,000 locations; each service session was invoiced at $29.95 for a total of $29,950. The invoices had a due date of March 10. Let's assume further that all of the office managers who received an invoice from Smith Tech Repair paid those invoices on March 10. Using cash accounting, Mr. Smith would record $0.00 in revenue for the month of February, even though he completed 1,000 service contracts; for March, he would record the paid invoices as $29,950 in income, even though the invoices were issued for work completed in February. Thus, cash accounting records income (and expenses) when is paid, not when it is earned (or incurred).

Using the same example, the accrual method of accounting would allow Mr. Smith to record $29,950 as income for the month of February, even though he will not receive the actual funds until March because the funds he received in March reflect income he earned from contracts that were completed in February. This aspect of accounting is known as the revenue recognition principle, which is discussed in greater detail in Chapters 5 and 12.

And as with income, so as with expenses. Let's say Smith had to hire an employee for the month of February to help him complete his service contracts. The employee worked for a total of 20 hours during the month of February, as a rate of $20 per hour. The employee earned $400 in February, and Smith Tech Repair issued a paycheck on March 10. This expense is recorded as a wages payable expense for the Month of February, even though the money does not leave Smith Tech Repair's bank account until March.

Accrual accounting also allows companies to distribute some types expenses over time. Let's assume that Mr. Smith pays $450 per month to rent his office and workspace. He pays the entire cost of annual rent at the beginning of every year, so each January, he writes the building manger a check for $5,400. The check is written and cashed in January, so using the cash accounting method, Mr. Smith would show a January rent expense of $5,400. However, the January rent expense really reflects costs that cover the entire year. By using the accrual method, Mr. Smith can show a rent expense of $450 per month, even though all of the money was paid in January. Thus, in both of these examples, the accrual method allows a company to record its expenses when they are incurred, rather than when they are paid. This principle is known as the matching principle, which is discussed in greater detail in Chapters 5 and 12.

By using the accrual method, the income statement provides a more accurate description of a company's profitability. Investors and financial regulators who examine income statements are less interested in the amount of cash a company received or spent during a given time. Instead, they want to know whether the company's core services are producing revenue, and if so, whether the revenue the company produces is greater than or less than the amount of expenses they must pay to stay in business. Because all businesses provide their services and incur expenses over time, only an accounting method that records transactions over time can provide an accurate assessment of profitability.

Components of an Income Statement

Aside from the accounting method used to create an income statement, an accountant must also know what kind of financial data should be provided on an income statement. As stated earlier, the income statement reports two major categories of financial data—revenues and expenses. However, revenues that are not the same as the total of all cash receipts and expenses may involve more than simply the total of all checks written to pay bills.

There are two methods of creating an income statement—the single-step method and the multiple-step method. We'll examine the single-step method first. Using the single-step method, and income statement reports four main categories of financial data:

- Revenues
- Expenses
- Gains
- Losses

At the bottom of the Income Statement is the so-called "bottom line," which shows the company's Net Income for the period indicated at the top of the Income statement. We'll begin this section with a brief overview of what each of these categories of financial data includes before examining specific differences in terminology in greater detail.

Revenue

First, the Revenue section shows all amounts earned by a company from both operating and non-operating activities:

- Operating revenue is all revenue in a reporting period earned from a company's main activities. For example, for a manufacturer, wholesaler, or retailer, their operating revenue will reflect the amount of money they earned during the reporting period from product sales. Alternatively, a business that provides services—such as computer or automotive repair or legal services—operating revenue will reflect the amount of money during the reporting period earned as a direct result of providing those services.

- Non-operating revenue is money that business earns as a result of activity that is secondary to its core activities. Whether a company sells goods or services or both, the non-operating revenue section reports all money earned as a result of activity that is secondary to selling goods and services. For example, is a business has placed money in an interest-bearing account, the interest earned would be recorded as non-operating revenue. Similarly, if a business owns rental properties, the rental payments would be reported as non-operating revenue. Other types of non-operating revenue include royalty payments for copyrights or income from advertising sources.

Expenses

Next, the Expenses section of an income statement includes both primary and secondary expenses:

- Primary expenses are all expenses incurred as a result of generating operating revenue. Primary expenses are generally grouped into the following four main categories:
  - Cost of Goods Sold (CoGS)
  - Selling, general, and administrative expenses (SG&A)
  - Depreciation and Amortization
  - Research and development (R&D)
  - The specific expenses themselves may cover a die range of primary operating business activity, such as:
  - Employee wages
  - Sales commissions
  - Utility payments for telephone, electricity, etc.
  - Transportation and maintenance
- Secondary expenses are all expenses incurred as a result of business activity that is not directly related to the business's main, core goods and services. Secondary expenses may include costs such as:
  - Interest payments on loans
  - Bank fees.

Gains and Losses

Finally the income statement also records Gains and Losses. Gains are a form of income and losses are a form of expense, but the income statements separate them out to show specifically how a company is either earning money or spending money. Gains and losses generally occur as a result of a one-time sale of some type of asset for an amount of money that is different from its "book value."

- Gains result from the sale of an asset such as a company van, a company-owned building like a warehouse, in which the company is able to sell the item for more than its current market value. Gains may also result from the sale of investment securities that result in a net profit over the purchase price.
- Losses also result for the sale of assets. For example, if a company is forced to sell a vehicle that was damaged, or lost money in the sale of an investment security, the result would be recorded as a loss on the income statement.

Thus, gains can be considered a form of revenue, and losses can be considered a form of expense. However, gains and losses different from both operating and non-operating revenue, as well as from primary and secondary expenses because they result from special, one-time transactions, rather than routine business activity. By providing a separate place for these data on the income statement, investors, managers, and financial regulators can more accurately assess a company's strengths and weaknesses in terms of its profitability.

Net Income

Finally, when all of the revenue, expenses, gains, and losses that a company has incurred are accurately recorded in the appropriate section of the income statement, the bottom line shows the total net income for that company for the period of time specified at the top of the statement. The formula for calculating a company's net income is:

Net Income = (Revenue + Gains) − (Expenses + Losses)

Format of an Income Statement

As with all financial statements, the financial data on an income statement must be presented according to the established conventions of the accounting profession. Generally a single-step income statement should report financial data in the following order:

- Revenues and Gains
- Expenses and Losses
- Net Income

Following is a very simple example of how a single-step income statement may be calculated:

ABC Goods and Services
Income Statement
For the Six Months Ending June 30, 2019

Revenues and Gains

	Sales Revenue	$150,000.00
	Intrest earned	$3,000.00
	Sale of assets	$2,500.00
	Total Revenue and Gains	$155,500.00

Expenses and Losses

	Cost of Goods Sold	$100,000.00
	Wages and Commissions	$10,000.00
	Office supplies	$1,000.00
	Utilities and rent	$2,500.00
	Interest paid	$750.00
	Loss from asset sale	$1,000.00
	Total expenses and losses	$115,250.00

Net income $40,250.00

Of course, not all income statement's use the single-step method. The multiple-step income statement allows for a more complex expression of the relationships among a company's revenue sources, expenses, gains, and losses by multiple calculations that involve several subtraction operations to arrive at the net income. The multiple-step income statement calculates separate totals for operating revenues and operating expenses, and for non-operating revenues, expenses, gains and losses. It also includes a section for gross profit; this figure expresses the difference between sales revenue and the cost of goods sold.

The multiple-step income statement uses three steps to arrive at the net income:

1. Calculate the gross profit
2. Calculate the operating income
3. Calculate the net income

These aspects of the multiple-step income statement are discussed in more detail in the next section. But first, the following simple example illustrates show a multiple-step income statement differs from a single-step income statement:

ABC Goods and Services
Income Statement
For the Six Months Ending June 30, 2019

Operating revenue
Sales			$150,000.00
Cost of Good Sales Revenue			$100,000.00
Gross profit			$50,000.00

Operating expenses
Sales expenses			
	Advertising	$2,250.00	
	Commissions and wages	$10,000.00	$12,250.00
Administrative expesnes			
	Office supplies	$1,000.00	
	Utilities and rent	$2,500.00	$3,500.00
Total operating expenses			$15,750.00
Operating income			$34,250.00

Non-operating income and expenses
Non-operating interest revenue	$750.00
Gain from asset sale	$3,000.00
Intrest expenses	-$500.00
Loss from asset sale	-$250.00
Total non-opertaing revenue and expenses	$3,000.00

Net income — $37,250.00

Understanding the Income Statement

The income statement provides a useful method for allowing managers, financial regulators, and potential investors with an opportunity to gauge the profitability of a company's operating activities. A single-step income statement provides simple and clear picture of how a company's revenues are earned, and whether they are generating enough revenue to earn a profit after paying expenses. A multiple-step income statement provides a far more explicit view of a company's income and expenses and is usually favored by large corporations, especially those who are required to submit financial statement to the SEC.

Like the balance sheet, the data included on a company's income statement can be used to generate many types of ratios and other calculations useful not only in determining opportunities to increase a company's current profitability, but also to determine a company's future potential for growth. This section examines the significance of information included in an income statement and how it can help managers and investors understand a company's operations.

Gross Profit and Cost of Goods Sold

Especially if your company is a retailer that buys goods wholesale then sells them for a profit, the Cost of Goods Sold, or CoGS, is the amount of money the company pays the wholesaler to purchase inventory. Of course, not all companies earn revenue by purchasing inventory wholesale then selling it for a profit at retail prices. Regardless, no matter what kind of business model you are operating, you should be able to indicate a CoGS on your income statement. For example, if your company manufactures and sells items of apparel, the raw materials, machinery, and wages you must pay for to produce finished items of clothing would be considered the CoGS. Service companies may also be able to claim billable hours and employee training as among their CoGS expenses. Thus, it is inaccurate to assume we can determine a company's profits simply by looking for the total revenue earned. This figure may be important, but the income statement shows a refined understanding of income and expense figures. Look at the example of the multiple-step income statement above. It shows a figure for Gross Profit under operating revenue. The gross profit is an unrefined estimate of a company's earnings over a period of time. The gross profit results from subtracting the CoGS from the total sales revenue.

Aside from serving as the initial calculation toward figuring the net income for the reporting period, the gross profit figures also serve another valuable purpose—they allow investors, managers, and regulators to monitor a company's gross margin. Sometimes used interchangeably with gross profit, the gross margin is actually gross profit expressed as a percentage. In the example above, the gross margin is 33% ($50,000/$150,000). Readers of financial reports may monitor a company's gross margin to determine whether they are sustaining their profitability.

Operating Income Vs. Net Income

As discussed earlier, operating income indicates the amount of income a company earns as a direct result of its core business functions. In the multiple-step income statement above, we can see that the operating income for ABC Goods and Service is $34,250 for the reporting period indicated. Notice that the operating income is different from the operating revenue. Operating income considers income not only net sales, but all financial activity related to core business. Using this example, the operating income is less than gross profit because it accounts for all the administrative and related expenses associated with running the business. Thus, the formula for Operating Income is Gross **Profit – Operating Expenses = Operating Income**.

Of course, larger corporations are usually involved in a wide variety of financial activity. Mergers and acquisitions; securities investments and reinvestment of revenue; asset purchases such as land, buildings, and vehicles; and many other types of financial activity may also generate income for a company. Smaller companies may also earn residual income from rental properties, investments in certificates of deposit, or interest earned on business checking and savings accounts. As a result, the operating income alone does not provide an accurate assessment of a company's total revenue.

The income statement above shows very clearly that ABC Goods and Services was able to generate an additional $3,000 in net revenue from non-operating activities. This information in itself is helpful to anyone seeking a clearer understanding of the company's financial standing by reading the income statement. But perhaps, more importantly, the income statement can be used to calculate a ratio between the net income and the operating income—the larger percentage that a company's net income results from operating income, the less the company is depending on financial activity not related to the core business. In the above example, 92% of the ABC's net income results from operating income; this high percentage can signal to investors that the company is not depending on outside investments to maintain profitability.

Retained Earnings and Dividends

The examples in this section provide a straightforward sample of the standard format and organization of information on an income statement. In the real world, a major global corporation will likely have a tremendous amount of financial activity that needs to be accounted for. A well-designed income statement may make all that accounting appear uncomplicated on the surface, but it is important to remember that financial statements represent the final product, not the potential arduous process of understanding where to place each type of financial transaction record.

The following image shows an income statement form Amazon, Inc:

AMAZON.COM, INC.
CONSOLIDATED STATEMENTS OF OPERATIONS
(in millions, except per share data)

	Year Ended December 31,		
	2015	2016	2017
Net product sales	$ 79,268	$ 94,665	$ 118,573
Net service sales	27,738	41,322	59,293
Total net sales	107,006	135,987	177,866
Operating expenses:			
Cost of sales	71,651	88,265	111,934
Fulfillment	13,410	17,619	25,249
Marketing	5,254	7,233	10,069
Technology and content	12,540	16,085	22,620
General and administrative	1,747	2,432	3,674
Other operating expense, net	171	167	214
Total operating expenses	104,773	131,801	173,760
Operating income	2,233	4,186	4,106
Interest income	50	100	202
Interest expense	(459)	(484)	(848)
Other income (expense), net	(256)	90	346
Total non-operating income (expense)	(665)	(294)	(300)
Income before income taxes	1,568	3,892	3,806
Provision for income taxes	(950)	(1,425)	(769)
Equity-method investment activity, net of tax	(22)	(96)	(4)
Net income	$ 596	$ 2,371	$ 3,033
Basic earnings per share	$ 1.28	$ 5.01	$ 6.32
Diluted earnings per share	$ 1.25	$ 4.90	$ 6.15
Weighted-average shares used in computation of earnings per share:			
Basic	467	474	480
Diluted	477	484	493

Using this example, we will consider two examples of how creating an income statement may require that you reconsider how you categorize certain forms of income and expense.

Retained Earnings Are Not the Same as Cash

First, it may be tempting to think of a company's Retained Earnings as simply another component of its revenues. If your company shows retained earnings on your balance sheet under Shareholders' Equity, you may look for a place to include this figure as part of your operating income—after all, logic dictates that all money earned as a result of core business activities should be included in operating revenue. However, while retained earnings result from revenue, they are not the same as cash. Retained earnings earned from revenue are those finds specifically designated for future use, usually to pay dividends to shareholders. As a result, a company's retained earnings are more closely related to their net income because it represents the net income a company saves over time.

In the above example, Amazon's net income for 2015 was $596 million; their retained earnings would be determined as a percentage of that net income that was held for future use.

Dividends Are Not an Expense

One of the most common uses of Retained Earnings is to pay dividends to shareholders. Whereas the first two examples in this section provided a clear illustration of how a company's net income is the difference between its gross profit and its operating expenses, plus any additional non-operating revenue (or losses). However, neither of these simpler examples discussed how income taxes and dividend payments also affect a company's bottom line.

Using the more realistic example of Amazon's income statement, notice that the figure for net income appears below the figure for "Income before income taxes." Thus, after all operating and non-operating expenses are accounted for, the Income Statement must also show how the actual net income will be affected by taxes. So, the net income is the result of subtracting the amount of income tax due from pre-tax income. But before this final amount can be carried forward to the Retained Earnings account, the amount for dividends due to shareholders must be deducted. Thus, dividends are not an expense of business operations, so much as a deduction from Retained Earnings.

Chapter 4: The Cash Flow Statement

Figure 5: Free Image

The cash flow statement is the third of the three main financial statements. (The other two are the balance sheet and the income statement, both of which are discussed in the preceding two chapters. In addition, some companies choose to also include a statement of stockholders' equity. You can read a definition of this fourth type of financial statements in the Glossary in Chapter 15). The cash flow statement is also known as the statement of cash flows or funds flow statement.

Like the income statement, the cash flow statement shows a company's financial condition over a specified period of time. The essential difference between the income statement and the cash flow statement is that the income statement shows whether a company is profitable; the cash flow statement shows whether a company is liquid. In other words, an income statement may tell you whether or not a company earned money or lost money during a given period of time, but a chase flow statement will show exactly how money was earned or spent. Cash flow statements separates the activities of a company into three main sections—operating activities, investing activities, and financing activities. In addition, there are two methods of generating a cash flow statement—the direct method, which is generally used with cash-based accounting systems and the indirect method, which utilizes accrual-based accounting and incorporates information from the balance statement and the income statement. This chapter discusses the specific features of a cash flow statement and how the information in cash flow statement may be used to evaluate a company's performance.

What is a Cash Flow Statement?

The cash flow statement is also known as the statement of cash flows or statement of funds flows. The cash flow statement bridges the gaps between the income statement and the balance sheet.

Remember that the income statement is created using the accrual method of accounting; thus, it reports not only revenue that has been received, but also revenue that has been earned and invoiced. Similarly, the income records all expenses—both those that have been billed and those that have been paid. Remember also that the balance sheet include both accounts receivable and accounts payable in its calculation of a company's total book value. In addition, the balance sheet indicates the company's value at one specific point in time.

Investors or financial regulators who wanted to make a determination about how much of a company's revenue had already been received and how much of that revenue resulted from cash transactions earned through operating activities, the core services of the business, could use the information included in the balance sheet and the income statement and then make adjustments to the figures to account for credit purchases, investment income, tax liabilities, etc. However, because the cash flow statement is designed with this goal in mind, many investors and creditors will simply request a cash flow statement to understand how the company manages its financial resources, where its money is coming from, how those funds are being spent, and whether the company has enough cash on hand to pay its current outstanding debt obligations. These determinations are difficult enough to assess by simply reviewing financial data. For this reason, the cash flow statement is always required as one of the three major types of financial statements.

The cash flow statement is separated into three main components:

- Cash earned from operating activities
- Cash earned from investing activities
- Cash earned from financing activities

In addition, a fourth component is sometimes included, particularly when cash flow statements are prepared according to the GAAP:

- Disclosure of noncash activities

These sections of the cash flow statement illustrates the important distinction between this type of report and the income statement and balance sheet. Specifically, the cash flow statement deliberately excludes the amount of future incoming and outgoing cash from transactions that have been recorded as credit. Thus, although net income provides an accurate assessment of how much money a company has made after all expenses are accounted for, net income is not the same as cash because it includes both cash and credit sales and expenses.

Cash flow statements may be used for a variety of reasons. For example, by comparing cash from operating activities to cash from net income, an investor can assess the quality of a company's earnings. Specifically, if cash income from operating activities is consistently higher than net income, then the company's earnings may be described as "high quality"; whereas, a company whose operating activities produce less than their net income may cause serious concern among investors. Second, for investors who believe that "cash is king," a cash flow statement can help investors see whether a company is generating more cash than it is using. Such companies will have greater resources to reinvest in the company, making them a more attractive prospect.

Adjusting Data for the Cash Flow Statement

The three sections at the end of this chapter discuss each of the components of the cash flow statement in turn. But before examining those aspects, this section discusses how the financial data in the balance sheet and the income statement are adjusted for the cash flow statement. Essentially, accountants will adjust balance sheet and income statement items to revenue, expenses, and credit using addition or subtraction. These adjustments allow accountants to reevaluate whether the totals on these two types of financial reports results for cash or non-cash transactions and whether they should appear on the cash flow statement.

The following sections discuss how some types of accounts are adjusted prior to their inclusion on the cash flow statement:

Accounts receivable

Accountants must evaluate the balances of accounts receivable sections of balance sheet for more than one period to make adjustments for the cash flow statement. For example, if the accounts receivable balance on a company's balance sheet for January is higher than the accounts receivable balance for the same company's balance sheet in June, this change indicates that more cash has entered the company as a result of customers paying their credit balances. In this case, the accountant will add the amount of the decrease to the total for net sales. On the other hand, if the accounts receivable balance for the same period increases, the amount of the increase is deducted from net sales to show the decrease in cash revenue.

Inventory

Assessing changes in inventory for inclusion on the cash flow statement are slightly more complex. An increase in inventory value on a company's balance sheet from one reporting period to the next indicates that company has spent money to purchase raw materials or wholesale goods. That increased value must be deducted from net sales, but only is the inventory was purchased with cash. Conversely, if the value of inventory decreases, the value of the decrease is added to net sales. However, if inventory was purchased with credit, the balance sheet will show an increase in accounts payable with a corresponding increase in the value of the inventory from one reporting period the next added to net sales.

Accounts payable

Whether the account is taxes payable, wages, payable, or prepaid expenses such as insurance, balances of accounts payable accounts that have been paid off from one reporting period to the next must be subtracted from net income. If accounts payable have not yet been paid off, any differences is in closing balances from one reporting period to the next must be added to net earnings.

Adjustment methods

Adjustments are made using one of two methods:
- Direct cash flow method
- Indirect cash flow method

Direct Cash Flow Method

The direct cash flow method uses actual cash flow data taken directly from a given company's operations and present cash flow data according to gross classifications of cash receipts and payments. For example, using the direct method, the accountant will gather all transaction records and cash receipts showing cash payments made to suppliers, cash receipts shoeing sales to customers, and records of salary payments to employees. Totals for inclusion on the cash flow statement result from calculating beginning and ending balances of the applicable accounts, then assessing the net increase or decrease in their value over the course of the applicable accounting period.

Indirect Cash Flow Method

The indirect method derives financial data from the balance sheet and the income statement and comparing changes in the various account types from one reporting period to the next. Both the balance sheet and the income statement are calculated using the accrual method, so certain adjustments have to be made to the totals to ensure they reflect only cash transactions. For example, because the net income figure on the income statement includes income that may have been earned but not yet received. As a result, the accountant must adjust for earnings before interest and taxes (EBIT) so he or she can isolate cash income and deduct amounts from accounts receivable. In addition, non-operating activities like depreciation that do not affect cash flow must also be included when using the indirect cash flow method.

Components of the Cash Flow Statement

Cash Flow from Operating Activities

The first section of the cash flow statement reports cash from operating activities. This section shows all cash payment received and all cash payments made by a company in support of its operating activities, which are all those business activities directly related to the daily maintenance of its core business functions. For example, for a hardware store, operating activities would include all sales of merchandise from the store's inventory, payment of employee wages, rent and utility payments for the store facility, and all tax and interest payments related to these activities. Other types of financial activity not directly related to operating activities are included in the other two sections of the cash flow statement—investing activities and financing activities. The following types of financial records result from operating activities:

- Cash receipts from sales of goods and services
- Interest payments
- Income tax payments
- Payments made to suppliers for inventory or raw materials used for production
- Salary and wage payments to employees

- Rent and utility payments
- Transportation costs directly related to operating activities
- Accounts Receivable
- Inventory
- Supplies
- Prepaid Insurance
- Accounts Payable
- Unearned Revenues
- Other Current Liabilities

Investment companies, whose goods and services are comprised entirely of securities and other financial products and services, may also include cash receipts for sales of loans or other debt and equity instruments.

Because operating activities represent the main source of a business's revenue generation, this section is generally considered to be the most important section of the cash flow statement. Positive cash flow over time indicates a company in healthy financial condition. The stronger the positive cash flow, the healthier the financial condition of the company. Financial data on the operating activities of a cash flow statement are reported in the following order:

- Net earnings (The net income figure taken directly from the income statement.)
- Additions to cash:

        - Depreciations
        - Decrease in accounts receivable
        - Increase in accounts payable
        - Increase in taxes payable
        - Etc.
    - Subtractions from cash:
        - Increase in inventory
        - Increase in accounts receivable
        - Decrease in accounts payable
        - Etc.
- Net cash from operations.

Cash Flow from Investing Activities

This section of the cash flow statement records changes in the value of equipment, fixed assets, or other financial instruments. Changes in cash flow resulting from investing activity records how much money has been spent or generated as a result of making investments during specified period of time.

Depending on the type, size, and complexity of your business, you may include some or all of these types of investment activities. There are many other types of investment activities not listed here that may also appear on your cash flow statement.

In addition, the following types of financial activity should NOT appear in the investing activities section of the cash flow statement:
- Interest payments
- Dividend payments
- Financing data related to debt or equity
- Depreciation of fixed assets
- Any income or expenses that are part of operating activities

Generally, transactions in this section of the cash flow statement are reported in the following order:
- Purchases of property, plant, and equipment (PP&E)
- Income from the sale of PP&E
- Purchases for the acquisition of other companies or businesses
- Income from the sale of other companies or businesses
- Purchases of investment securities, such as stocks and bonds
- Income from the sale of investment securities

Cash Flow from Financing Activities

Finally, this section of the cash flow statement records changes in long-term liability and stockholders' equity, such as debt, loans, stock options, and other forms of financing, from one reporting period to the next. Any company that needs to raise money must do so using equity (by issuing shares) or debt (by taking out loans). Changes to both new and existing financing activities will be shown on the cash flow statement.

Whereas the operating activities section shows how much net cash a company has generated over time, and the investing activities section shows how that company has spent the money it has generated, the financing activities section shows how a company funds its overall operations.

The following types of accounts may be included in the financing activities section of the cash flow statement:
- Issuance of equity
- Repayment of equity
- Dividend payments
- Issuance of debt through new loans
- Debt repayment

- Lease payments on capital investments
- Bonds Payable
- Deferred Income Taxes
- Preferred Stock
- Paid-in Capital in Excess of Par-Preferred Stock
- Common Stock
- Paid-in Capital in Excess of Par-Common Stock
- Paid-in Capital from Treasury Stock
- Retained Earnings
- Treasury Stock

In this section of the cash flow statement, activities are recorded as an inflow of cash when capital is raised and as an outflow of cash when dividends are paid. For example, if a company issues bonds for public purchase, the company will revive cash when investors purchase the bonds; however, the company must also pay interest to the bondholders, which results in a cash outflow in this section of the cash flow statement.

Generally, financial data in this section of the cash flow statement is reported in the following order:
- Income received from issuing long-term debt
- Cash outflow for repayment of long-term debt
- Cash outflow for principal repayments of capital lease obligations

- Cash outflow for principal repayments of finance lease obligations

Sample Cash Flow Statement

The following illustration provides a simple example of how cash statement illustrates changes in the cash value of the different areas of a company's business activities over time. The top figure shows an example of a cash flow statement that uses the direct method, and the bottom figure shows a cash flow statement that uses the indirect method. Notice how the primary difference in these two statements is that the figures for operating activities using the direct method are derived directly from the business daily transactions; whereas, the operating activities section using the indirect method requires a refinement of data taken from the balance sheet and income statement.

Direct Method:
    Operating Activities
        Cash received from customers $800
        Cash paid to suppliers   (150)
        Employee compensations   (200)
        Other operating expenses paid   (250)
        Net cash from operating activities   200
    Investing Activities
        Sale of land   200
        Purchase of equipment   (300)
        Net cash from investing activities   (100)
    Financing Activities
        Common share dividends   (200)
        Payment on long-term debt   (300)
        Net cash from financing activities   (500)
    Beginning Cash Balance   X
    Ending Cash Balance   Y

Indirect Method:
    Operating Activities
        Net Income $50,000
        Add: Depreciation expense $10,000
        Decrease in AR $2,000
        Increase in inventory $3,000
        Decrease in prepaid expense $4,000
        Increase in accounts payable $5,000
        Net Cash provided by operating activities $XXX
    Investing Activities
        Sale of land   200
        Purchase of equipment   (300)
        Net cash from investing activities   (100)
    Financing Activities
        Common share dividends   (200)
        Payment on long-term debt   (300)
        Net cash from financing activities   (500)
    Beginning Cash Balance   X
    Ending Cash Balance   Y

Chapter 5: Generally Accepted Accounting Principles

Figure 6: Free Image

Generally Accepted Accounting Principles—or GAAP—is a term used to describe a set of rules and standards that govern the accounting profession. Consider the vast number of privately and publicly held businesses in operation on any given day. From small, local retail and service businesses, to medium-sized companies that operate in more than one city or state to major multinational corporations, the variations in the types of goods and services offered and the complex demands and needs of investors and other interested parties require some type of standardized financial reporting. If each company simply maintained and produced accounting records and reports according to its own individually developed accounting techniques and philosophies, investors, banks, managers and financial regulators would have to spend more time trying to understand each company's accounting and bookkeeping methods than the information actually contained in their financial statements.

The GAAP govern the practice of accounting in three major areas: basic accounting principles and guidelines, rules and standards determined by the Financial Standards Accounting Board (FASB), and generally accepted industry practices that have evolved over time. The FASB, the Securities and Exchange Commission (SEC), the American Institute of CPAs (AICPA), and the Governmental Accounting Standards Board (GASB) all contribute to the rules and standards of the GAAP. The GASB and the FAF, in turn, are administered by the Financial Accounting Foundation (FAF). The GAAP is used primarily with the United States. Internationally, companies usually conform to the International Financial Reporting Standards (IFRS). This chapter discusses some of the specifics relating to each of these regulatory agencies, the various principles included under the GAAP, and the differences between the GAAP and the IFRS.

What Are Generally Accepted Accounting Principles (GAAP)?

The GAAP are concepts, principles, and conventions that govern the format and content of financial statements. Depending on the size and complexity of the business, the laws of the United States may require a company to release these financial statements on a regular basis and submit them to regulatory agencies such as the SEC. The ten principles of the GAAP are:

- Principle of regularity: To maintain compliance with the GAAP, financial statements accountants and their financial statements must always demonstrate strict adherence to established regulations.
- Principle of consistency: All accounting standards apply to all entities throughout the financial reporting process.
- Principle of sincerity: Accountants must be committed to producing financial statements that are accurate, impartial, and free of bias or conflict of interest.
- Principle of permanence of methods: GAAP-compliant accountants must adhere consistently to the same uniform set of procedures to prepare financial reports and statements.

- Principle of non-compensation: All financial statements, must report complete coverage of off all a business entity's transactions. Positive reports must be produced free of inducements through compensation or reward; negative reports must be produced free of the fear of retaliation or sanction.
- Principle of prudence: GAAP-compliant accountants may not allow speculation to influence their reporting of financial data.
- Principle of continuity: GAAP-compliant financial statements that include asset valuations assume that the organization's operations will continue.
- Principle of periodicity: GAAP-compliant accountants must report revenues according to standard accounting time periods, such as fiscal quarters or fiscal years.
- Principle of materiality: All GAAP-compliant financial reports must fully disclose an organization's financial condition.
- Principle of utmost good faith: All parties involved in the production of GAAP-compliant financial statements will be assumed to be acting with complete honesty.

Who are the SEC, the AICPA, the FASB and the GASB?

All of these organizations are financial regulatory agencies administered either by the federal government or by independent advisory boards. Each of them has a specific concentration, and all of them work together to ensure that all business transactions and financial activity are conducted according to established principles and methods and according to laws. These organizations not only work with governmental law-making, they may also have the authority to enforce laws, investigate complaints of criminal activity, impose sanctions and other penalties against businesses who operate outside the law or fail to comply with established standards. Together, ensure stability and legal compliance in business and financial transactions and dealings. This section provides a brief overview of each of these agencies in turn, including the degree to which they contribute to the formation and enforcement of the GAAP.

Securities and Exchange Commission

The Securities and Exchange Commission—the SEC—is an agency within the federal government of the United States of America. The official mission of the SEC is "to protect investors; maintain fair, orderly, and efficient markets; and facilitate capital formation. The SEC strives to promote a market environment that is worthy of the public's trust" (About the Division of Enforcement, 2007). The SEC has seven major divisions:

- Corporation Finance
- Enforcement
- Investment Management
- Economic and Risk Analysis
- Trading and Markets
- Office of Administrative Law Judges
- Office of Compliance Inspections and Examinations

All of these divisions share responsibility for enforcing laws that affect both domestic and international business transactions, particularly investment transactions. The Division of Corporation Finance, in particular, has issued recent rulings governing the use of GAAP accounting principles in financial statements released to investors. A recent release from April 2018 entitled, "Non-GAAP Financial Measures," provides the SEC's detailed responses to the types of financial statements that may violate certain laws enforced by the SEC if they do not comply with GAAP principles.

The American Institute of Certified Public Accountants (AICPA)

The AICPA was founded in 1897 to represent the interests of the accounting profession. Since its founding, the accounting profession has been an established and recognized force in ensuring this field is regulated by rigorous educational requirements, high professional standards, a strict adherence to ethical conduct and a commitment to serving the public interest.

As a certification body, the AICPA develops and grades performance on the Uniform CPA Examination. As a regulatory agency, the AICPA monitors and enforces compliance with the standards of the accounting profession.

Today, the AICPA provides advocacy services for the accounting profession before legislative bodies, public interest groups and other professional associations. In addition, the AICPA is responsible for developing standards and rules for conducting audits of private companies, as well as many of the other responsibilities of professional CPAs. The AICPA also provides educational material and guidance for members.

The Financial Accounting Standards Board (FASB)

The FASB was founded in 1973. The FASB is a non-profit private-sector regulatory agency with headquarters in Norwalk, CT. The FASB's main function is to establish the accounting and reporting standards for all companies—whether public sector or private sector—and all non-profit organizations that adhere to GAAP. Both the SEC and the AICPA have recognized the authority of the FASB. The SEC regards the FASB as the official regulatory body overseeing the accounting standards of public companies.

The FASB operates in cooperation with the Financial Accounting Foundation (FAF) and the Governmental Accounting Standards Board (GASB). The FAF is also an independent, private-sector, non-profit organization and oversees the administration of both the FASB and the GASB. Together with the FAF and the GASB, the FASB's mission is to ensure that financial accounting and reporting standards are upheld and that investors and other stakeholders have access to understand how those standards apply.

The Governmental Accounting Standards Board (GASB)

The GASB was established in 1984. Also based in Norwalk, CT, and also an independent, private-sector, non-profit organization, the GASB establishes accounting and financial reporting standards for American state and local governments agencies that adhere to the GAAP.

The GASB's authority as a regulatory body is recognized by the AICPS, as well as state and local governments and state boards of accountancy. The GASB develops accounting standards in collaboration with the FASB and the FAF. The FAF also oversees the administration, financing, and appointments within the GASB.

Differences Between U.S. Accounting Standards and International Accounting Standards

The GAAP accounting framework is used predominantly by companies and organizations that operate within the United States. Publicly held companies within the United States that are regulated by the SEC may be required to issue GAAP-compliant financial statements. Other companies may choose to conform to GAAP accounting standards as a means of establishing trust among investors and other interested parties. The GAAP have been codified into the Accounting Standards Codification (ASC), the official statement of GAAP policy issued by the FASB.

Although the GAAP is recognized internationally, most countries outside the United States use the International Financial Reporting Standards (IFRS) framework. Whereas the GAAP is heavily dependent on complex and detailed rules, the IFRS focus is on general principles. As a result, IFRS documentation is a much smaller body of legislative work that then the GAAP. Although the IFRS as a result is easier to understand and potentially easier to apply than the GAAP, the GAAP is regarded as for more comprehensive.

Currently, some regulatory agencies are making an effort to bridge gaps between these two accounting frameworks, with an eventual goal of reducing the number and complexity of differences. Although some regulatory bodies believe the two frameworks should eventually be merged, others have voiced dissent leading to the significant possibility that these frameworks will remain separate and independent.

Chapter 6: Double-Entry Accounting

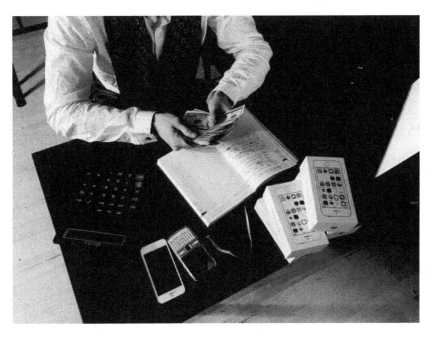

Figure 7: Free Image

Double-entry accounting uses a system of recording transactions that requires two entries for every transaction—one entry shows where money came from; the other entry shows where money went. These entries are called debits and credits, and for every transaction, the total amount debited muse be the same as the total amount credited. Because two entries are required for every transaction, it is called double-entry accounting. The counterpart of double-entry accounting is single-entry accounting. Most people who manage their personal finances—as when balancing their checkbook when paying their monthly household expenses—use single-entry accounting. With single-entry accounting, only one entry is required for each transaction—if you make a deposit to your savings account, you simply write in the amount of the deposit and update the balance; if you write a check to pay a bill, you simply write the amount of the check and deduct it from the balance in your account. Most people don't consider that there is a second part of these transactions—in the first example, the money you placed in your savings account had to come from somewhere, and in the second example, although you decreased the balance in your checking account, you also decreased the total amount you own in bills for the month. Double-entry accounting requires the accountant to ensure that both sides of every transaction are recorded. The result is a more accurate picture of money management, and financial statements that contain a more detailed analysis of a company's financial condition.

Understanding the general principle of double-entry accounting is easy enough. In actual practice, there are considerable complexities, and you may have to relearn some of the terminology you have grown accustomed to—especially the use of the terms, "debit" and "credit." However, with a little diligence and patience, anyone can learn to use the double-entry system of accounting. In addition, because double-entry accounting is generally required for adherence to GAAP standards, learning to use this system earlier rather than later can help your business succeed. This chapter covers several important aspects of double-entry accounting, including debits and credits, general journal entries, general ledger entries, and the trial balance.

Debits and Credits

Before considering debits and credits themselves, consider that accounting groups all transactions into separate accounts. Chapters 1, 2, and 3 discussed the basics of accounting from a general perspective. Chapter 1 discussed that all of the accounts used to record a business's daily transactions are listed in the chart of accounts. Chapter 4 discussed how the balance sheet shows all of the accounts that comprise a company's assets, liabilities, and equity. Chapter 3 discussed how the income statement incorporates in accounts resulting from revenue, expenses, gains, and losses. Thus, however many individual accounts may be listed on a chart of accounts, all those individual accounts will fall into one of seven categories:

- Assets
- Liabilities
- Equities
- Revenue
- Expenses
- Gains
- Losses

In accounting, a debit does not always decrease the balance of an account, and a credit does not always increase the balance of an account. Instead, debits are transaction entries placed on the left side of an account ledger, and credits are transaction entries placed on the right side of an account ledger. (The next sections discuss journals and ledgers in more detail.) Whether a debit or a credit either decreases or increases the balance of an account depends on which of the seven types of accounts listed above has been either debited or credited. For example, debiting an asset account increases the balance, but debiting either a liability or equity account decreases the balance. However, regardless of the type of account, the total debits and credits for every single transaction must be equal.

The following two charts will help you remember how debits and credits affect the various types of accounts:

Account Type	Increased By	Decreased By
Assets	Debit	Credit
Expenses	Debit	Credit
Liabilities	Credit	Debit
Equity	Credit	Debit
Revenue	Credit	Debit

Debits	Credits
Increase asset and expense accounts	Increase liability, equity, and revenue accounts
Decrease liability, equity, and revenue accounts	Decrease asset and expense accounts
Always recorded on the left side of the ledger	Always recorded on the right side of the account ledger

Examples of double-entry accounting

To use double-entry accounting accurately and effectively, the accountant must be able to determine which accounts are affected by every transaction. Every transaction involves money leaving one account, and money being added to another account. As a result, when an accountant records a transaction, he or she must be able to determine which account the money was taken from and which account money was taken and into which account money was deposited for the transaction to have been completed.

Let's suppose a mobile tech repair business purchase a fleet vans for its service technicians. The company purchased the vans on credit, and spent a total of $300,000. These vans have an estimated useful life of at least 10 years, so they are considered a fixed asset. An accountant using single-entry accounting might simply add the total purchase price to the outstanding balance of the company's line of credit. However, using double-entry accounting, the accountant must determine the cash inflow and the cash outflow, both of which must be equal.

In this example, the total value of the vans—$300,000—represents an increase to the company's assets account, so the accountant will debit assets for $300,000. At the same time, because the purchase was made on credit, the outflow of cash to purchase the new asset will be shown as an increased liability by crediting the accounts payable account for $300,000. Thus, although the debit and credit were applied to different accounts, the total amount of debits and credits for this transaction is equal—$300,000 for each.

The General Journal

The next question is, "Where are all these double-entry account transactions recorded?" The answer is that there are two places where business transactions are recorded—the general journal and the general ledger.

To begin, a general journal is sometimes referred to as the book of original entry because the journal is where the bookkeeper will record every daily transaction before the accountant processes the transaction information to produce financial reports. The next section discusses general ledgers in more detail, but suffice it to say here that the accountant depends on the journals as the source of information that is transferred into the ledger.

There is one very important fundamental difference between the journal and the leger—transactions in a journal are recorded chronologically, with every page organized into columns featuring transaction dates, serial numbers, transaction descriptions, account names, and debit and credit amounts.

Some companies will maintain specialized journals—for example to record only credit sales. These journals are usually created to assist in the efficiency of recording high-volume transactions. This section will limit the discussion to general journals.

A general journal may be used to record a wide variety of transactions, including asset sales, interest income, interest expense, cash or credit sales to customers, or operating expenses. To provide an illustration of how journals are used to record transactions, we'll construct an example.

- On February 3, a company purchases $2,500 in office supplies using the company credit card.
- On February 4, the company makes a credit sale of $3,750 to one customer and a cash sale of $4,250 to another customer.
- On February 5, the company ships the orders to both customers.
- On February 6, the company receives payment for the credit sale of February 4 and sends a check to the bank for the balance of the credit card bill.

Here is how the accounts might be recorded in a journal:

ABC Company
Journal for 20YY

Date	Account	Debit	Credit
03-Feb-20YY	130 Supplies Inventory	2,500	
	200 Accounts payable		2,500
04-Feb-20YY	105 Accounts Receivable	3,750	
	405 Sales Revenue		3,750
04-Feb-20YY	101 Cash	4,250	
	405 Sales Revenue		4,250

05-Feb-20YY	505 Cost of Goods Sold	8,000	
	120 Product Inventory		8,000
06-Feb-20YY	101 Cash	3,750	
	105 Accounts Receivable		3,750
06-Feb-20YY	200 Accounts Payable	2,500	
	101 Cash		2,500

Notice several important aspects of these journal entries:
- All transactions are listed chronologically
- Every debit entry is paired with a matching credit entry
- Debits are listed on the left; credits are listed on the right
- The sum of all the debit entries equals the sum of all the credit entries

These transaction entries represent bookkeeping—the first step of the accounting cycle. Although they are an invaluable record of the company's financial activity, the journal entries themselves are unhelpful in determining whether the company is generating a profit or any of the other insights for which financial statements are created. For this reason, the accountant must transfer the journal entries must be transferred into the general ledger. The next section discusses how to record entries in the general ledger.

The General Ledger

Unlike transaction records in journals that are recorded by date, transaction records in the general ledger are recorded by account. Another difference is that journal entire are entered across a page, from left to right. A standard, GAAP-compliant ledger entry uses a "T-account" format, which you can see in the following diagram. (In accounting, Dr. is the established method of abbreviating "debit; and Cr. is the established method of abbreviating "credit.")

Dr.			Cash Account		Cr.
Date	Description	Amount	Date	Description	Amount

The general ledger is the complete record of all accounts and transactions of a company. There will be a ledger page for every account listed in the chart of accounts. Many types of ledgers are available—loose-leaf binders, bound volumes, and electronic databases within computer programs.

Each specific account within a ledger will belong to one of several main categories. In addition, each of those categories is normally assigned a range of numbers, which can be used to numerically identify each of the accounts within each category. Accounts are usually are arranged in the following order:

- Assets (100-199)
- Liabilities (200-299)
- Equity (300-399)
- Revenues (400-499)

- Expenses (500-599)

Using the sample journal entries in the previous illustration, you can see that the cash account, accounts receivable, product inventory, and supplies inventory have been assigned account numbers 101, 105, 120 and 130, respectively, which make them all asset accounts. Accounts payable has been assigned account number 200, which makes it a liability account, and sales revenue has been assigned account number 405, which makes it a revenue account and cost of goods sold has been assigned account number 505, which makes it an expense account.

After the bookkeeper has entered all the daily transactions for a business into the journal, the accountant will post those transactions to the appropriate account within the ledger. The accounting term for recording transactions in ledger is "posting." Generally, accountants will post accounts from the journal to the ledger at specified time intervals, usually at the end of every month.

At the end of the accounting cycle, the accountant will total all the debits and credits in the ledger and transfer them to the trial balance.

The next section discusses the trial balance in greater detail, so for now we will use an example to illustrate how journal entries are transactions are posted to a ledger. We'll use the six journal entries from the example in the previous section to show how journal entries are posted to ledger accounts. In the following examples, each of the accounts listed in the journal entries represents an individual ledger account. Each ledger accounts starts with an opening balance on the first day of the month. As entries are posted to the ledger account from the journal, the balance is either increased or decreased. Notice that some types of accounts normally carry a debit balance; others normally carry a credit balance. Refer to the chart in the Debits and Credits section to see the effect of debit entries and credit entries on each account type.

Acct. 101	Cash		
Date	Debits	Credits	Dr. Balance
01-Feb-20YY			2,000
04-Feb-20YY	4,250		6,250
06-Feb-20YY	3,750	2,500	7,500

Acct. 105	Accounts Receivable		
Date	Debits	Credits	Dr. Balance
01-Feb-20YY			2,500
04-Feb-20YY	3,750		6,250
06-Feb-20YY		3,750	2,500

Acct. 120	Product Inventory		
Date	Debits	Credits	Dr. Balance
01-Feb-20YY			50,000
05-Feb-20YY		5,000	45,000

Acct. 130	Supplies Inventory		
Date	Debits	Credits	Dr. Balance
01-Feb-20YY			10,000
03-Feb-20YY	2,500		12,500

Acct. 200	Accounts Payable		
Date	Debits	Credits	Cr. Balance
01-Feb-20YY			1,200
03-Feb-20YY		2,500	3,700
06-Feb-20YY	2,500		1,200

Acct. 405		Sales Revenue	
Date	Debits	Credits	Cr. Balance
01-Feb-20YY			38,000
04-Feb-20YY		3,750	41,750
04-Feb-20YY		4,250	46,000

Acct. 505		Cost of Goods Sold	
Date	Debits	Credits	Dr. Balance
01-Feb-20YY			15,000
05-Feb-20YY	8,000		23,000

Notice several important aspects of these ledger entries:

- All transactions are organized by account first, then chronologically
- Account balances are updated with every entry
- Debits are listed on the left; credits are listed on the right
- The sum of all the debit entries equals the sum of all the credit entries

At the end of the accounting cycle or reporting period, the accountant will transfer all the debit and credit totals for all the accounts in the ledger to the trial balance worksheet. The next section discusses this process in more detail.

The Trial Balance

Chapter 1 discussed the six steps of the accounting cycle:
1. Analyzing and recording transactions
2. Posting transactions to the ledger
3. Preparing a trial balance
4. Preparing adjusting entries
5. Preparing an adjusted trial balance
6. Preparing financial statements

So far, this chapter has discussed the first two steps in detail: recording transactions in the journal and posting journal entries to the ledger. This section focuses on Step 3: preparing a trial balance. The trial balance was developed as a method for allowing the accountant to check for errors in the ledger and/or the journal before preparing financial statements. (Steps 4 and 5 provide a means for correcting any errors; and the last step is the creation of the statements themselves.)

The trial balance is not only one of the most important steps of the accounting cycle; it also highlights the true value of the double-entry system of accounting. Specifically, by providing a very direct method of comparing the total credits to the total debits entered into the account ledger for any given accounting period, the trial balance allows the accountant to spit potential errors that may have occurred either when the bookkeeper recorded transactions in the journal or when those entries were posted to the ledger.

Generally, accounting software is more effective at preventing errors before this stage than manual accounting because accounting software utilizes error-checking throughout the entire process of recording transactions. In addition, the trial balance is not the only method that an accountant should use to check for errors. This section will discuss error-checking after we examine a sample trial balance.

To create trial balance worksheet, the accountant must:

1. transfer all of the accounts from the chart of accounts to the trial balance worksheet;
2. transfer the closing debit or credit balances from each account in the ledger to the appropriate account on the trial balance worksheet;
3. total all of the debt balances and all of the credit balances.

Then, if the totals of the debit balances and credit balances are the same, the books are balanced, and the accountant can move to the next step.

But first, there are three important points to remember:

1. The following types of accounts normally carry debit balances:
    a. Asset accounts
    b. Expenses accounts
2. The following types of accounts normally carry credit balances:
    a. Liability accounts
    b. Equity accounts
    c. Revenue accounts
3. The trial balance does require the accountant to add every single debt and credit for every type of account; instead, the trial balance includes the closing balances for each account as listed in the account ledger.

The following example of a trial balance worksheet uses the same example from the previous two sections. Seven of the accounts were used specifically in the examples in the previous 2 sections. Some additional accounts have been added for illustration purposes. It is possible for an accountant to include closing balances for accounts in which there were no recorded transactions during the accounting period. Every company's chart of accounts is different. This example illustrates that all of a company's accounts will be included on the trial balance worksheet, not just those for which transactions have been recorded.

Account Number	Account for ABC Company Fiscal Year 20YY	Debit Balance	Credit Balance
Asset Accounts			
101	Cash	7,500	
105	Accounts Receivable	2,500	
120	Product Inventory	45,000	
103	Supplies	12,500	

	Inventory		
Liability Accounts			
200	**Accounts Payable**		**1,200**
205	Payroll Payable		5,250
Equity Accounts			
301	Owner's capital		20,000
320	Retained earnings		13,000
Revenue Accounts			
405	**Sales Revenue**		**46,000**
410	Service Sales Revenue		7,550
Expense Accounts			
505	**Cost of Goods Sold**	**23,000**	

510		2,500	
	Totals	93,000	93,000

Using the trial balance to check for errors

In this example, the closing balances of all accounts are equal. Notice that the closing accounts of the accounts in bold are transferred directly from the closing balances in the sample ledger entries in the previous section. The closing balances will reflect the difference to the opening balance resulting from the sum of all debits and credits posted to that account, so there is no reason for the accountant to add all the debits and credits individually.

If the totals at the bottom of the debt and credit columns do not match, there may be several reasons, including:

- An account balance may appear on the trial balance worksheet as a debit balance when it should be a credit balance (or vice-versa).
- The account balances may be incorrect as a result of a transposition error in one or more of the account balances figures.
- A debit or credit balance from one single account may have been omitted.

However, the trial balance may not detect certain types of accounting errors, such as:

- Incorrect values for debit or credit balances that do not result in unequal debt and credit balance totals.
- Transactions that were not entered into the journal.
- A transaction may have been entered as a credit, when it should have been entered as a debit.
- A transaction may have been posted to the wrong type of account.
- Two errors that offset each other may escape detection using only the trial balance worksheet.

A company's annual report and financial statements will be released to shareholders, tax authorities, financial regulators, bond and credit rating forms, and lenders. These statements may also require passage of an examination by auditors. As a result, accuracy in reporting accounting figures is vitally important to the ongoing success of a company's operations. Thus, regardless of whether the accounting error is purely mathematical or the result of more serious or complicated problems during the accounting cycle, creating the trial balance is a very important part of accurate accounting.

Chapter 7: Cash Accounting vs. Accrual Accounting

Figure 8: Free Image

The previous chapter noted the difference between single-entry and double-entry accounting. This chapter discusses another pair of comparable accounting methods—cash-based accounting and accrual accounting. The primary difference between these two methods consists entirely in when the funds involved in a transaction are recorded. When using cash accounting, transactions are recorded when they are paid for. When using the accrual method, transactions are corded at the time the transaction occurs, regardless of whether they are paid for at that time or later. There are many reasons a business would choose one accounting method over another. Generally, smaller businesses and individuals keeping track of their personal finances use cash accounting, while businesses with a larger volume of transactions and more complex operations use accrual accounting. Each method has particular strengths and weaknesses and in any given situation, one method may be preferable to another.

This chapter discusses in detail the fundamental differences between these two accounting methods. It also discusses how some expenses may be reported differently when using one method versus the other, and how that can affect a company's financial statements.

The Cash Method

Cash accounting recognizes revenue only when cash is received and expenses only when they are paid. As a result, a cash accounting system will not use accounts payable or accounts receivable accounts. Many small businesses may use a cash accounting system for a variety of reasons:

- Cash accounting allows for the implementation of a simple and easy to use accounting and bookkeeping system.

- Small companies that do not have to submit financial statements to the SEC or to shareholders may not require a more complex system of bookkeeping and accounting.

- Using a cash accounting system makes it easier to determine whether a payment has been received or paid by simply confirming whether the money has either been deposited or withdrawn from the bank. There is no need to review invoices and accounts payable to track outstanding bills or pending payments.

- Using a cash accounting system allows for a very straightforward method of establishing the value of a company's cash account by simply checking the current bank balance.

- Companies that employ cash accounting do not have to pay taxes of revenue they have not yet received.

The Accrual Method

Accrual accounting recognizes revenue when it is earned and expenses when they are incurred, regardless of when the money is either deposited in or withdrawn from the bank. For example, let's say a customer buys a service contract from a company, and the company completes the service agreements and sends the customer an invoice. Although the customer doesn't pay the invoice for 30 days, the company records the income as revenue at the time the contract is signed. Similarly, if a company buys $2,000 in office supplies using the company credit card, the expense is recorded at the time of purchase, even if the bill isn't paid for another 30 days or longer.

The accrual method is a more common accounting method for several reasons. Primarily, the accrual method provides the company with a means to more accurately assess its income and expenses over time. Whereas the cash method allows any company to determine its cash on hand simply be checking the bank balance, the accrual method allows company to add in revenue it has earned but not received and subtract expenses it has or will incur but has not yet paid. As a result using accrual accounting can be beneficial to budget planning and essential when compiling financial statements. However, accrual accounting can also convey a false impression of profitability if it relies too heavily on accounts receivable and not enough on the value of its cash accounts. This inability to gauge cash flow can have serious consequences if a company incurs too many expenses without having the cash to pay for them.

The following chart summarizes the advantages and disadvantages of both accounting methods.

Cash Method	Accrual Method
Recognizes revenue only when cash is received	Recognizes revenue at the time it is earned, regardless of when goods and services are paid for.

Recognizes expenses only when cash leaves the bank.	Recognizes expenses at the time they are incurred, regardless of when they are paid for.
Cash revenue that has not yet been received cannot be taxed.	All revenue (including accounts payable) is taxable in the reporting period in which it was earned.
More common among small businesses that do not maintain a sales inventory.	Required for all businesses that generate $5 million or more.

Examples of Cash vs. Accrual Accounting

This section provides real-world examples of how cash accounting methods differ from accrual accounting methods using two specific types of transactions: prepaid expenses and unearned revenue.

- Let's say Company XYZ rents a manufacturing facility where it manufactures and sells goods to retail customers. The company pays $1,000 per month to rent its manufacturing facility.

- On December 2, the company manager receives the rental invoice for the upcoming month of January.
- The company manager signed a one-year lease agreement with the property manager.
- On December 3, the manager decides to pay all the rent for the upcoming year in one lump sum and sends a check for $12,000 to the property manager. The property manager cashes the check the same day.
- On December 7, the company receives two orders—one for $8,000 worth of goods, the other for $4,000 worth of goods. Both customers sent payment in full with their order requests.
- On December 7, the company deposits the payments for both orders into the company checking account.
- On December 8, the company delivers the first order for $4,000.
- The second order requires additional manufacturing and will not be ready for shipment until January 5.

Now, we will examine how these transactions will be recorded using both the cash method and the accrual method.

Prepaid Expenses

Company ABC pays $12,000 per year in rent to do business out of its facility. In this case, the manager paid all the rent for the following year (2020) in December 2019. Using the cash accounting method, he will record a transaction in the daily journal for the month of December for $12,000.

Using the accrual method, he will be able to take advantage of the matching principle, which allows him to allocate prepaid expenses over time. In this case, although he paid $12,000 in the month of December, he will not record any of those funds as a rental expense for December. Instead, he will record $1,000 in the general journal for each month of the upcoming year; those entries will be posted to the Rental Expense account in the general ledger, again for each month of the upcoming year.

The difference in accounting methods for prepaid expenses can affect a company's financial statement dramatically.

Using the cash method, this company's balance sheet will show a $12,000 expense for the month of December. In addition, this amount must be deducted from their annual revenue. Although the larger deduction for rent in December may allow them to pay less in taxes, their cash flow statement will not reflect an accurate picture because all of the rent for the year 2020 will have appeared on the cash flow statement for 2019, and monthly expenses for 2020 will not reflect rental expenses because the money changed hands in December 2019.

Using the accrual method, the company spends $12,000 in cash in December, but none of it is recorded as an expense for December because the money is used to pay rental expenses for 2020. The company will not be able to deduct the $12,000 as an expense on their taxes for 2019. However, their balance sheet and their cash flow statement will reflect their financial condition more accurately—not only will the $12,000 rental expenses be distributed evenly across all the months for the 2020 fiscal year; neither their balance statement nor their cash flow statement for 2019 will reflect the $12,000 expense.

Unearned Revenue

Company ABC received $12,000 in revenue in December for two orders. Using the cash method of accounting, all of that revenue will be recorded for the month of December and must be reported as income on their taxes. However, only $4,000 of the total amount sold has been delivered. As a result, the company must pay taxes in 2019 for income it has not yet earned; in addition, their balance sheet cannot reflect unearned income as a liability to offset the costs in labor to produce the remaining $8,000 in goods. As a result, it will reflect assets it has not yet earned, resulting in an inaccurate portrayal of their current financial condition.

Using the accrual method, the company can record the $4,000 in revenue it earned in December and record the $8,000 for the second order in the Unearned Revenue account under Liabilities. The accountant can also enter the amount of material and labor required to produce and ship the send order by crediting the supplies inventory and debiting the wages payable accounts. As a result, the company can defer taxation for the $8,000 in unearned revenue to the following year and produce financial statements that reflect a more accurate picture of their financial condition.

Other types of transactions

Because every transaction is different and may involve many different types of accounts, the specific differences, advantages, and disadvantages between recording those accounts using either the cash or accrual method may vary widely. However, the IRS requires that all businesses indicate withtype of accounting method they are suing. Changing accounting methods requires that the company file Form 3115.

Chapter 8: Depreciation of Fixed Assets

Everyone is familiar with the concept that when you buy a brand new car, it loses several thousand dollars in value as soon as you drive it off the dealer's lot. This decline in value is known as depreciation. Depreciation is also an accounting method that can help businesses mitigate the cost of major investments by reporting the amount of value of their fixed assets lose over time. Not all assets should be depreciated—for example, even though the new recycle bin you purchased for your office will be around for a long time, its relatively low cost make the prospect of depreciating it more trouble than it would be worth. However, major purchases such as office equipment, computers, manufacturing equipment, buildings, vehicles, and storage facilities will definitely require a major investment of capital. Using GAAP-compliant methods of depreciation, a business can deduct the cost of purchasing the asset accurately. By using this opportunity to report the purchase as a business expense, a company can reduce its taxable income, resulting in a lower tax bill, which can compensate for the initial cost of purchasing the asset.

There are specific rules governing the use of depreciation. There are also several different types of depreciation methods, including straight-line, declining balance, double declining balance, sum-of-the-year's digits, and units of production. This chapter first discusses straight-line depreciation in detail, with brief descriptions of the other types of depreciation. It also discusses the concepts of accumulated depreciation, salvage value, and net gain or loss on a sale.

Straight-line Depreciation

Put simply, depreciation is used to match the cost of a given fixed asset with the amount of revenue it generates, which allows a company to record revenues and expenses used to produce them together in the same accounting period in which they occur. Depreciation allows the accountant to show the gradual decline of the ability of the proportionate ability of the asset to produce the associated amount of revenue. By using depreciation, the financial statements provide a more accurate record of the company's financial condition and capacity to generate revenue.

Because it is almost impossible to directly link the exact amount of revenue generated with the cost of a fixed asset, established methods of depreciation instead utilize several standardized techniques and valuation methods to identify the asset's useful life and calculate its declining value over that period.

Straight-line depreciation is the standard method of calculating this figure. Straight-line depreciation is used when there is no established pattern of how an asset will be used over time, so it uses a basic formula that can be applied to any fixed asset used for any purpose under any conditions. Straight-line depreciation is also the easiest method, so there are fewer opportunities accounting errors. Following are the six steps used to calculate straight-line depreciation:

1. Determine the initial cost of the fixed asset to be depreciated.
2. Determine the salvage value of the asset.
3. Subtract the estimated salvage value of the asset from the purchase cost of the asset, as recorded in the ledger.
4. Determine an estimated useful life for the asset. Often, each type of fixed asset will have a standard useful life already assigned to it for accounting purposes; this estimate should be used wherever possible.

5. Divide the number of years of the estimated useful life into 1. This is the straight-line depreciation rate.

6. Multiply the depreciation rate by the asset cost (less salvage value).

Step-by-step Straight-line Depreciation

The following example shows how straight-line depreciation can be used to record the expense of purchasing new fixed assets.

1. Let's say Company ABC purchased a packaging machine for $50,000. The machine has an expected useful life of 15 years and an estimated salvage value of $10,000. The depreciation rate can be calculated as follows:

    a. Depreciation rate = 1/Years of useful life
        i. Depreciation rate = 1/15 0.066
        ii. Depreciation rate = 0.066
        iii. Depreciation rate = 6.7%
    b. Asset cost (50,000) − Salvage value (10,000) = $40,000
    c. Adjusted asset cost ($40,000) x Depreciation rate (6.7%) = $2,680 per year.

2. Next, to record the expense for purchasing this new fixed asset using depreciation, they do not have to record an expense of $50,000 at the time of purchase, even if they paid $50,000 cash. Instead, the company record the expense as follows:

    a. Record $2,680 against net income for the first year.

    b. Record $2,680 in depreciation expense for every following for the next 14 years.

    c. After 15 years, sell the asset for the estimated salvage value of $10,000 and record any net gain or loss on the sale.

Accumulated Depreciation

Accumulated depreciation is an asset account that appears in a company's chart of accounts. The accumulated depreciation account is used to record the total depreciation of a fixed asset for the time it was first purchased and made available for use. Because the accumulated depreciation account is a contra account, it normally carries a credit balance even though it is an asset account. As a result, the accountant will report accumulated depreciation on the balance sheet as a reduction in the gross value of fixed assets.

Over the life of the asset, the balance of the accumulated depreciation account for an asset will increase, as the value of its depreciation is recorded each year. The amount of accumulated depreciation can be subtracted from the original purchase cost of the asset, or gross cost, to calculate the asset's carrying amount.

When the asset is sold at the end of its useful life, the balance of the accumulated depreciation account is reversed along with the original purchase price of the asset. This method of derecognition of the asset is completely removes it from the company's books to avoid retaining values for gross fixed assets and accumulated depreciation.

Using the example in the previous section, the following journal entries show how depreciation and derecognition would be recorded. First, the annual entry for depreciation of the packaging machine would be entered in the journal like this:

	Debit	Credit
Depreciation expense	2,680	
Accumulated depreciation		2680

After 15 years, the asset will be sold for the salvage value, so the following entry will be recorded to purge the accumulated depreciation account:

	Debit	Credit
Accumulated depreciation	40,200	
Fixed assets		40,200

Journal entries will be posted to the ledger and then to the trial balance at the conclusion of each accounting period prior to issuing financial statements. The next two sections discuss salvage value and net gains or losses on the sale of an asset.

Salvage Value

As discussed in previous sections, the salvage is the estimated value of an asset at the end of its estimated useful life. Some companies may have an established method of estimating the salvage value of certain asset types, and most companies have devised internal methods that accounting departments employ when calculating salvage value. Regardless of the method of calculating the salvage, it is important to establish that value at the time the asset is purchased because it will affect the annual depreciation charge and should be the same as the carrying value of the depreciated asset at the end of its useful life.

To calculate the salvage value, a company will take many factors into consideration. For instance, if a company believes a particular asset will have a long useful life and will contribute demonstrably to the company's revenue, the useful life of the asset will be much longer, and the salvage value may also be correspondingly lower. On the other hand, a company may be less optimistic about an asset's ability to contribute to revenue over time. As a result, the company may assign the asset a much shorter useful life with a much higher salvage value. Alternatively, using accelerated depreciation instead of straight-line depreciation can allow a company to deduct greater depreciation earlier in the asset's useful life prior to selling it for its estimated salvage value.

Unfortunately, the largely unregulated area of salvage valuation had led some accountants to use this figure in a fraudulent manner. For example, if a fixed asset is assigned an artificially high salvage value, the annual depreciation may considerably lower, making it possible to report higher profits than were actually earned. Chapter 13 discusses fraud and ethics in greater detail.

Gain or Loss on Sale

The net gain or loss on the sale of an asset is recorded after an asset has reached the end of its useful life. Often, the salvage value will simply be the amount for which a company believes it will be able to sell the asset at the end of its useful life. In such cases, the closer amount received for selling the asset at the end of its useful life, the lower the net gain or loss will be recorded for. Either way, in deal circumstances, the income generated from the sale of an asset will be enough to compensate for the final carrying amount of the asset at the end of the depreciation period. If the company receives more than the salvage value recorded on the books, it records a net gain. If it receives less, it records a net loss.

Many companies may routinely depreciate an asset to a salvage value of $0 if they believe it will have minimal value at the end of its useful life, or if they believe its only salvage value will be a result of selling the asset for parts. In these cases, the entire purchase price of the asset is depreciated annually, and any proceeds from selling the asset at the end of its useful life are recorded as a net gain.

Chapter 9: Amortization of Intangible Assets

Amortization is an accounting method whereby a company can show the costs associated with acquiring intangible assets. Chapter 8 discusses the process of depreciating fixed assets over time to provide a method of accounting for major purchases as business expenses. The costs associated with tangible, fixed assets such as furniture, machinery, buildings and vehicles—all physical objects that lose value as a result of normal wear and tear and usage over time—are accounted for through the use of depreciation. However, intangible assets, such as copyrights and trademarks, pose a different challenge to a company's accounting department. These assets are fundamentally different from fixed assets, so accounting for the costs associated with acquiring them also requires a different method.

There are many assets that may fall under the category of intangible assets. Accounts must also make several determinations when they are considering how to amortize an intangible asset. This chapter provides a detailed discussion of amortization, including a list of categories and types of intangible assets, how to use amortization to account for their value and some of the terms related to amortization.

What Are Intangible Assets?

Defining intangible assets can be a challenge. Although the concept itself is fairly easy to understand, in terms of accounting, additional considerations include whether the asset meets certain criteria and whether the intangible asset is eligible for amortization.

1. First, intangible assets are all assets owned by a company that are not physical objects or cannot otherwise be physically touched. The following fairly comprehensive list identifies many types of intangible assets:
   - Registered trademarks
   - Customer and client lists
   - Franchise agreements
   - Computer software copyrights
   - Patents
   - Brand names

- Logos
- Domain names
- Artistic assets, including photos, videos, paintings, films, and audio recordings
- Defensive assets acquired to prevent others from using it—for example, buying and registering an internet domain to prevent another company from using the same or a similar company name.
- Any other forms of intellectual property
- Business licenses
- Leasehold improvements, in which a landlord takes ownership of the improvements
- Proprietary software developed for internal use
- Goodwill, which is defined as the purchase price of a business entity that has been sold to another business entity, less the amount of the value not already assigned to specifically identified assets and liabilities that were acquired as a result of the acquisition.

2. To be considered an intangible asset, the asset must meet all the following criteria:
- It must be a non-physical asset.
- It must provide value to the company.
- Its benefit to the company must be in the form of a measurable effect, such as cost.

- The cost of preparing an intangible asset must be attributable to its intended use. For instance, when a company purchases a patent, it must be for the intended use of protecting patent rights for something the company invented.
- Intangible assets resulting from development may be recognized as intangible assets only if their use or sale generate future benefits, if the expenses attributed to the intangible asset can be measured, and if the company has enough resources to complete the development of the asset.

3. To qualify for amortization, an intangible asset must have a useful life of more than one year. In addition, although there are many assets that may be considered intangible asset, not all types of intangible assets can be amortized. For example, the following types of intangible assets may be amortized:

- Patents
- Copyrights
- Trademarks
- Intellectual Property
- Franchise rights
- Business licenses

On the other hand, the following types of intangible assets may not be amortized:

- Goodwill (except for private companies)

- Brand names
- Logos
- Publishing titles
- Customer lists

Straight-line Amortization

Amortization of intangible assets is an accounting process that allows companies to distribute the expenses associated with acquiring the asset over the projected life of the asset. In this way, amortization is similar to depreciation. An accountant may record different amortization values depending on whether the values are for corporate accounting purposes or for tax purposes—amortization for tax purposes requires costs to be distributed over a specific number of years regardless of the actual useful life of the asset.

As with depreciation, there are several established methods of amortization methods These methods include the straight-line method, the diminishing balance method, the unit of production method, the declining balance method, and the double-declining balance method. This section will focus on the straight-line method of amortization.

Amortizing an intangible asset using the straight-line method can be accomplished in four steps. To amortize an intangible asset:

1. Determine the start date.

   Generally, the start date of an intangible asset is the date it was first purchased, acquired, or made available for use. For example:
   - The start date for patent is the date on which it was purchased or for which it was applied.
   - The start date of a copyright is the date it was issued.
   - The start date of a business license is the date it was obtained.

2. Determine the initial cost of the intangible asset.

   Generally, this will simply be the amount of money spent to acquire the asset. For example if a patent application required a $75,000 purchase fee, then $75,000 is the initial cost of the intangible asset. The costs required to develop the invention cannot be included.

   Intangible assets that are initially developed internally, such as software developments and leasehold improvements, should be recognized at their actual cost. Any other intangible assets that are developed internally should be charged to expense in the period in which the expense is incurred.

3. Calculate the estimated useful life of the asset.

We'll use the same example as in the previous step. If the patent purchased by the company for $75,000 protects the invention for 20 years, then this is the useful life of the intangible asset.

4. Calculate the amortization.

The formula for calculating straight-line amortization is:

Initial Cost/Useful Life = Annual Amortization Value

Using the same example of the $75,000 patent, the amortization value will be calculated as follows:

$75,000/20=$3750

Legal Life vs. Expected Useful Life

One of the fundamental differences between intangible assets and fixed assets is that fixed assets typically have salvage value. The corresponding terms for salvage value as applied to intangible assets is residual value. But most intangible assets generally do not have any residual value—their entire cost can be amortized. The previous example of the patent originally had an expected useful life of 20 years; in this case, this may be expressed as its legal life, since it expires legally after the initial 20-year period of protection.

Although intangible assets rarely have residual value, it is usually advisable to conduct impairment testing to determine whether the intangible asset's carrying value may become unrecoverable—that is, if the legal or expected useful life of the intangible asset is shortened considerably, resulting in the need to write off the remaining value of the amortization. The useful life of an intangible asset may change over time. Using the example above, the 20-year patent may protect a technological invention. However, if new technology renders the invention obsolete in ten years, the useful life of the patent expires early, and the remaining value may be written off. Other changes that may reduce or annul the legal or expected useful life of an intangible asset include:

- A significant decrease in the market price of the asset
- Any significant adverse change in the manner in which the asset is used, which damages or lessens its value
- Any significant adverse change in either the legal factors or the controlling business climate that govern the use of the asset
- Any unexpected and excessive costs incurred by the company during the process of acquiring or developing the asset
- Any operating or cash flow losses associated with the asset

- Any use of the asset that results in a likelihood of greater than 50% that it will be sold or otherwise disposed of before the end of its estimated useful life

In any of these cases, the accountant must recognize an impairment loss by debiting an impairment loss account and crediting the intangible assets account. The new carrying amount of the intangible asset will be it most recent carrying amount, less the amount of the impairment loss. In addition, amortization for the remainder of the intangible asset's expected useful life may have to be recalculated using the remaining useful life and any change to the value of the asset itself.

Chapter 10: Inventory and Cost of Goods Sold (CoGS)

For retail businesses, the inventory is likely its most important asset. A retail business generates revenue mainly be selling products to customers. While there are many other assets a retail business may depend on—its point-of-sale machines and cash registers, the facilities and buildings where its stores are housed, storage facilities, shipping materials, and in-store displays—without merchandise to sell, there would be no business to conduct.

Closely related to inventory is the Cost of Goods Sold (CoGS). Whereas inventory is an asset, CoGS is an expense. Many businesses simply buy merchandise from wholesalers and manufacturers, then sell it to retail customers. Other businesses buy the raw materials from suppliers, manufacture their inventory from the raw materials, then sell the end products to retail consumers through their stores.

Regardless of the specific details of the business model, inventory and CoGS may be the largest and most important asset and expense, respectively, of any retail business. These two financial concerns are also closely related in terms of reporting performance on financial statements. This chapter discusses in detail how to account for both inventory and CoGS, including the perpetual method, the periodic method and how to calculate to CoGS.

Inventory

Depending on the type and size of any given business, ordering and maintaining inventory can be a key aspect of that business's success. Any business that relies on the sale of merchandise as its main source of revenue must have an inventory of items readily available for its customers to purchase. A company must first purchase inventory from the wholesaler or manufacturer. This purchase is recorded as an expense known as Cost of Goods Sold. Once the inventory items have been received, they are recorded as an asset. Inventory is considered an asset on the balance sheet of a business, and they can only be expensed as they are sold to customers.

A business will indicate its beginning inventory on its income statement. Beginning inventory is the value of all the inventory that is left over from the previous year. As the new fiscal year begins, additional inventory purchases are added to this balance. At the end of the year, the value of all the products that were not sold are subtracted from the beginning inventory plus the value of any additional purchases. The result ids the Cost of Goods Sold (CoGS). This chapter discusses CoGS in the final section, but the intimal focus is on inventory.

The importance of accounting for inventory cannot be stressed enough. Inventory is reported as an asset of the balance sheet, but unlike may fixed assets or financial assets like cash or securities, inventory must be very closely monitored. A business that has too much inventory may encounter cash flow problems if they spent too much on purchasing items for resale. They may also run into additional expenses, such as storage and insurance. They can also encounter losses if the inventory becomes obsolete. On the other hand, a company that has too little inventory may lose revenue from lost sales. Because of the importance of inventory to the success of a retail business, the accounting profession has established specific methods for recording and managing inventory.

Perpetual Method

The perpetual method is a more sophisticated and far more widely used method of recording inventory. The perpetual method is more expensive than the periodic method, mostly because it requires the use of extensive technology and staff to maintain. The perpetual system is so-named because it keeps track of inventory balances of all inventory items on a continual, ongoing basis. When new inventory items are purchased by the business, they are entered into the company's computer system. As items are sold throughout the day, the company's accounting software records the sale of the item and automatically updates the inventory balance. Assuming there is no theft or damage, and assuming there is no human error regarding data input into the computerized inventory tracking software, a perpetual inventory account balance should reflect an accurate, real-time balance of any item and of all items included in the business's inventory.

To understand what a perpetual inventory system looks like in action, consider purchasing items at a grocery store. When scanned at the cash register during checkout, the barcode stamped on the item not only tell the customer and the clerk how much the items costs, but also instantly updates that total in the inventory account balances.

Especially in the modern business environment, a perpetual inventory system is a must for large businesses with high sales volumes, particularly if the business operates as a chain with many franchises in many locations. A perpetual inventory system allows these types of businesses offers advantages, such as checking for errors related to inventory, providing a comprehensive list of all transactions down the level of individual items sold. Managers can also make more informed decisions about purchasing and can more easily identify problems related to theft.

However, due to their complexity and cost, perpetual inventory systems are not right for every type of business.

Periodic Method

The periodic method of inventory requires an occasional physical count of all inventory items. Physical counts are compared against beginning inventory values to measure the relative value of existing inventory, CoGS, and what types of purchases are required to bring inventory counts to desired levels.

Business owners that use the periodic method to update inventory values at the end of set periods throughout the fiscal year—once a month, once every quarter, or annually. All purchases to restock inventory are recorded in the company's purchase account. After the inventory has been counted, the balances in the purchase account are transferred to the inventory account. The inventory account is adjusted at the end of each reporting period to account for ending balances.

- Using a periodic system, the CoGS is calculated using the following formulas:
- Beginning inventory + Purchases = Total cost of inventory (goods)
- Total cost of inventory − Ending inventory = Total cost of goods sold

The following table compares aspects of perpetual and periodic inventory systems:

	Perpetual Method	Periodic Method
Accounts	General ledger updates occur automatically	Account updates only occur after inventory counts

Technology	Businesses with many locations that conduct thousands of transactions a day cannot maintain physical counts of inventory. They are dependent on technology.	Simple manual recordkeeping of small inventories is still possible.
CoGS	Account balances are continuously and automatically updated as each sale is recorded.	The value is calculated at the end of the reporting period using the formula shown above.
Cycle counting	Cycle counts can be automatically generated.	Cycle counts are not possible because inventory is not tracked in real time.

Purchases	New inventory purchases are automatically recorded and accounts balances are automatically updated.	All purchases are recorded into the purchase account manually.
Error-checking	Error checking is fairly easy by configuring search parameters suing the software.	Error checking is extremely difficult, because unit-level tracking is not employed in the periodic system.

Calculating Cost of Goods Sold

The Cost of Goods Sold (CoGS) is closely related to inventory. Whereas inventory is recorded as an asset on a company's balance sheet, CoGSis reported as an expense. Depending on the type of business, CoGS may include several costs:

- For retailers that purchase items wholesale, the CoGS will include the entire purchase price the business paid to the supplier.

163

- For businesses that manufacture goods for sale, CoGs will include the cost of purchasing the raw materials needed to manufacture the items.
- CoGS may also include all the costs associated with preparing items for sale to customers, such as shipping, labor, manufacturing overhead, etc.

The following formula is used to calculate the CoGS:

- CoGS = Beginning Inventory + P − Ending Inventory

(P indicates purchases during the accounting cycle.) CoGS is an important part of a company's financial statements. A company's gross profits are determined by subtracting the COGS from revenue. Gross profits, in turn, provide an indication of a company's profitability. When a company's CoGS increases, its net income will decrease and understanding this relationship is useful for inventors and financial regulators.

CoGS Methods

As there are different methods of recording inventory balances, so there are different methods of calculating CoGS. The value of CoGS depends upon the method used by the business. There are three methods a company may use when recording inventory levels to arrive a t a value of CoGS: First In, First Out; Last In, Last Out (LIFO); and the Average Cost method.

- **First-In First-Out Method (FIFO)**

Using this method, the inventory goods that were purchased earliest are sold first. Generally, prices for all goods tend to increase over time, so companies using FIFO will sell items for which it paid a lower price first. Bey selling its least expensive items first, the CoGs for the reporting period will be lower, resulting in a higher net income over time.

- **Last-In First-Out Method (LIFO)**

Using this inventory method, the inventory items that a company purchased at the latest date are sold first. Again, because the cost of most items tends to increase over time, calculating CoGS according to this method generally results in higher CoGS value at the end of the reporting period, thereby resulting in a lower reported net income.

- **Average Cost Method**

Finally, the Average cost method simply averages the purchase cost of all of the same type of items currently held in a company's inventory, regardless of purchase date. This method generally cancels out changes in the purchase price of inventory items over time. As a result, the CoGS figure is not as heavily impacted by significant costs related to a single purchase or series of purchases. Net income figures are much more stable when using this system.

Chapter 11: Budgeting for Your Business

Figure 9: Free Image

If you have ever been responsible for paying any kind of bill for any kind of household expense, you have at least some experience in budgeting. Usually, whenever someone receives a bill for a credit card or other service, such as gas, electricity or telephone, the first question that runs through your mind is, "Do I have enough money to pay this bill?" After thinking about the balance in your checking account, other bills you may have recently received, and any events you may have planned for the weekend, you'll answer either yes or no. If your answer is no, you will likely begin thinking of ways to come up with money to pay the bill. This aspect of money management is part of budgeting, although this example illustrates budgeting practices that are far from ideal.

Business budgeting is the practice of considers all the time, money and resources available, then formulating a plan for how to manage operations in such a way as to use all available resources to a maximum advantage. Depending on the size and complexity of your business, the amount of resources available to you, the current economic climate and your goals and objectives for growth, the budgeting process can range from routine and relatively straightforward to arduous, painstaking and extremely challenging. Regardless, running a business without some type of budget is not a good practice. Fortunately, established business using professional accounting practices have developed many standardized forms of business budgeting, so you will not have to completely invent a process from scratch. This chapter discusses many of the complexities of professional commercial budgeting, including a general overview, budget planning and control, the advantages of budgeting and the many different types of budgets.

What is Budgeting?

In simple terms, a budget is a financial plan for future activities. Whereas, your home budget may include allocations of money for vacation, utilities, mortgage or rent, and groceries, a business budget will be concerned with such priorities as production, inventory, sales and capital expenditures.

A well-designed budget can help a business decide which areas of growth it will pursue, and what resources it will use to do so. In addition, a budget can be an indispensable yardstick when compared to a balance sheet and can help a business determine how well it managed to stay on course with its plans for revenue and growth.

Alternatively, a budget can help businesses that are experiencing slow growth or expenses that seem too high find ways to trim spending and reallocate resources in an effort to return operations to a more profitable path. By identifying variances—i.e., differences between actual expenditures and budgeted costs—managers can pinpoint where resources may need to be reined in.

Regardless of the type of budget, all of them will likely share four basic characteristics:

1. Show management's specific plans for the coming fiscal periods;

2. Provide specific numeric allocations of resources for achieving those goals;
3. Require all levels of management to engage actively in conscious debate and decision-making about the direction of the company;
4. Motivate management and staff toward achieving the goals in the budget.

Planning and Control

- **Planning**

Planning and control are two fundamental aspects of the budget process. Every budget is, by definition, a plan. Depending on the size and complexity of a business, the resources it may have available for use, and the current economic climate, a budget planning session may range anywhere from very simple to extremely complex.

This chapter discusses the many types of budgets that are in wide use in a later section. However, most budget plans will include at the very least a projected income statement with forecasts for expected growth. More complex budget planning may include considerations for the specific components and division of a company's operations, including sales forecasts, inventory purchases, fixed asset purchases. Still others will even include detailed cash flow statements indicating exactly how retained earnings should be spent, how much should be allocated for investing in new equipment and an estimate of how much financing may be required.

The larger and more complex the organization, the greater number of budget and the more details should be included in each one. In cases where organizations require several budgets to cover all areas of operations, the company should also create a master budget that contains a summary of all budgeting items, with details for individual components more specific departments.

Budgets can also vary in terms of the length of time for which they will be in effect. There are drawbacks to using long-term budgets because no budget, regardless of how thorough, can ever account for every possible change or event. In such cases, intermittent budget planning meetings may be required to make updates and adjustments to existing budgets.

Many companies simply use electronic spreadsheet software, like Microsoft Excel, to compose, post, and distribute budgets. Most software of this type is sufficiently powerful to handle even complex mathematical formulas for creating accurate projections of costs and revenue. However, may companies will purchase software designed specifically for creating budgets. There may be a variety of reasons for choosing such applications, including automatic error-checking, a lower possibility of mathematical errors, ease of use, or specific functions that enable budgeting for extremely complex or highly specialized financing needs.

A primary reason many organizations hold budget planning session is to establish a baseline against which the company can measure its future performance. This use of a budget may require frequent updates to account for unforeseen changes, but any adjustments to the budget should be made to ensure the comparison to the original baseline is as accurate as possible, rather than to retro-fit actual results to reflect an artificially optimistic comparison to the baseline.

- ## Control

Although budget planning is an indispensable step in the eventual creation of a usable budget, without effective controls most budgets will likely remain nothing more than a detailed list of intentions and aspirations. If budget planning can be compared to mapping out a travel route, budget controls represent the tools and agreed methods the navigator will use during the journey to ensure a safe arrival.

Once the budget has been issued, budgetary controls are used to ensure that all spending, purchasing, and management decisions are made in an effort to realize the goals stated in the budget. Management may employ many techniques throughout any given fiscal cycle to monitor progress throughout the period. When deviations and variances are detected, management will have the knowledge to step in and make changes to restore business activity to the plan of action laid out in the budget.

Performance measure controls

Consider the enormous array of resources available to an accounting department—particularly an accounting department that utilizes accounting software—to assess any division of a company's operations. By using the established principles of accounting and well-kept records, an accountant can make a determination at any given time exactly how well a company has maintained adherence to objective established in the budget.

- By periodically checking budgeted amounts for sales revenues with current balances, the company can pinpoint bottlenecks to find where inefficiencies or business failures may be occurring.
- By reviewing budget models for part of sales or manufacturing processes that are costing value, budgeting controls can ensure that necessary expenditures are allocated to accommodate increased volume.
- Using the final budget model for performance appraisals can improve motivation among staff to reach goals.
- Creating separate budgets for all responsible parties can increase the sense of autonomy and also improve motivation.

Accuracy and error-checking

Budgeting controls can also be implemented during the planning stages to ensure budgets are created with maximum efficiency and clarity and a minimum of errors. For example:

- By creating budgets for groups of employees, companies can dramatically reduce the number of line items in a budget.
- Managers may be more likely to make errors in budget models, so requesting that accountants design pre-filled templates can cut costs associated with revisions.
- Manually checking budgets for errors, with a final round of budget reviews by the entire budget planning team everyone can help companies avoid long-term losses.
- Using all available security measures to ensure the final budget is protected from unauthorized access.
- Using tracking logs can make meetings to discuss changes to the budget effective and more efficient.

Advantages of Budgeting

Some companies choose to operate without a budget to avoid the costs and frustrations of complex budget planning sessions. Operating without a budget can be risky and requires ongoing short-term forecasts to ensure the company has enough cash to continue paying its bills and fund operations. With enough discipline and attention, operating without a budget can be an effective method of management.

However, most businesses find that having a budget in place is a more advantageous method of managing operations. Following are five specific advantages to maintaining an operation budget:

1. Businesses can coordinate their activities more effectively.
2. Managers have better awareness of the operating plans for other managers in other departments.
3. Employees who are made aware of the specific details of budget see themselves as a more integral part of the business and become more highly motivated and more conscious about their use of resources.
4. A budget provides a company with a concrete method for reviewing its organizational plans, which makes implementing changes more

feasible and increases the likelihood that they will lead to success.

5. Managers who participate in budget planning will be inspired to foster a vision for the company that may otherwise have gone unnoticed or undiscovered.

Different Types of Budgets

Most of this chapter has discussed budgets in general terms. To some degree it is necessary to discuss budgeting in general terms because the specific goals, needs, and resources of any business will be vastly different from every other business. Budgets, too, will be similarly unique, so trying to provide universally applicable budget templates does not serve any practical purpose.

However, this section will provide a brief overview of the many types of budgets most businesses use throughout the accounting cycle.

To begin, most companies will formulate two types of budgets:
- operational budgets
- capital budgets

Operational budgets provide projected spending and revenue goals for all the various aspects of a company's operating activities—the core functions of the business. These types of budgets may include projected revenue, expenditures, and other allocations for any of the following operating activities:

- projections for sales revenue
- projections for production of goods
- amounts allocated to each department for expenses
- a master budget that summarizes all of the operational budgets and includes a master profit plan
- a cash budget that incorporates cash receipts and disbursements
- projected financial statements that will be compared to the financial statements issued at the end of the accounting cycle

Other types of operational budgets may include:

- materials budgets
- manufacturing budgets
- administrative cost budgets
- plant utilization budgets
- research and development budgets

In addition, any of these budgets may use any of the following budgeting styles:

- fixed or static budgets, which is not adjusted or changed over the course of the budget cycle
- flexible budgets, which allow for changes and adjustments in response to changes in volume or activity
- rolling budgets (also known as continuous or perpetual budgets) which provides management with a budget that looks ahead one full accounting cycle

After completing budget planning meetings and the approval process, operational budgets are used as the detailed roadmap for the business's operational activities in the next fiscal cycle. Capital budgets account for activities that may not be directly related to operational activities and that may overlap several accounting cycles. Capital budgets are less concerned with the day-to-day operations of a business and focus instead on major projects and capital expenditures for fixed assets. A capital budget will generally consist of a detailed listing of each project, with the specific amounts allocated for each project and the projected revenue they are expected to generate. These types of budgets may also rank projects according to their priority and expected profitability. Capital budgets are sued as the roadmap not only for investments in fixed assets in future fiscal cycles, but also how the financing for these projects will be arranged.

Chapter 12: Important Principles and Conventions of Accounting

Figure 10: Free Image

Chapter 5 of this book discusses the GAAP and the regulatory agencies that assume responsibility for ensuring that financial statements are issued according to established standards. Your business may use accounting software, or perhaps you have outsourced your bookkeeping and accounting responsibilities or hired a private accountant to maintain your books for you. As a result, because of the collective knowledge of agencies that enforce the GAAP and the skills of professional accounting services, you may not consider as important whether you have a firm grasp of the underlying assumptions of the accounting profession. However, making good business decisions requires the ability to interpret your company's financial statements independently and to make and follow-through on decisions based on quality financial intelligence. Even if your accountant make recommendations about budgeting and investment, that advice is only as valuable as far as you are able to understand why your accountant has made those recommendations and how implementing can help your business grow and thrive.

By taking some time to consider some of the important principles and conventions of accounting, you can become a better business manager and can help your business enter the phase of growth and prosperity you hoped for at founding. This chapter explores many of the most important fundamental accounting principles and provides an overview of many other principles and conventions.

Learning to Classify Different Accounts

Much of this book has discussed many of the methods and practices employed by professional accountants to ensure the records of business transactions they are responsible for recording are reliable and reflect an accurate picture of the company's financial condition at any given point in time, and comparatively over consecutive reporting periods.

Double-entry accounting, in particular, was developed to ensure that accountants had a reliable means of checking for errors prior to closing the books and producing financial statements. Accounting software has made error-checking easier because most programs will alert users to errors as they enter data and will not accept inaccurate or unbalanced entries to journals or ledgers.

The accuracy and reliability of accounting data depends particularly on one aspect of accounting—ensuring that you have classified the income or expense correctly and have debited or credited the right type of account. Remember that there are five major types of account classifications:

Asset accounts. Asset accounts are things of value that a company owns. Using the accrual method of accounting, assets may include not only cash on hand, but accounts receivable that representative money you have already earned, but that the customer has not yet paid.

Liability accounts. These accounts to some degree are the opposite of asset accounts. Liabilities are financial obligations—bills the company owns for payments on loans or mortgages. If an account is a liability account, if often ends with the word "payable," rather than "receivables."

Owner's or shareholders' equity accounts. These accounts represent capital—cash, stock, or real estate—that offset the amount of money the company owes in liabilities. If all a company's liabilities are subtracted from its assets, the remaining value is the owner's equity—how much of the business's value that is in the owner's possession. If the company is publicly traded, these accounts are known as shareholders' equity accounts. The main account in this type of category is the Retained Earnings account. This account records the amount of sales revenue a company retinas and reinvests back in the business.

Revenue accounts. These accounts record two types of transactions—revenue resulting from operating activities, which are the core functions of any given business—and revenue resulting from non-operating activities such as investments and income from rental payments on buildings owned by the business.

Expense accounts. Any type of expenditure made to support the operating and non-operating activities of a business can be considered an expense. There may be many types of expenses accounts, such as office supplies, or utility and rental payments.

The accuracy of a company's financial records depends not only on ensuring that the amount of every transaction is recorded correctly, but that each transaction is attributed to the right type of account. For example, accounting errors will be reflected in the trial balance prior to generating financial statements if debits and credits are attributed to liability or expense accounts when they should be attributed to asset or revenue accounts. Double-entry accounting provides for very reliable and thorough financial reporting system, but only if it is used as intended. The following section provides a brief overview of many accounting principles that are essential to effective accounting and bookkeeping.

The Business Entity Principle

This accounting principle assumes that all of the transaction information recorded in journals and ledgers that eventually comprise the data in financial statements is derived exclusively from the financial activity of a recognized business entity, separate from its owners' personal financial activity, and separate from the financial activity of other business entities.

The Monetary Unit Principle

The monetary unit principle assumes that all of a company's financial activities will be expressed in terms of monetary units. Whether the accountant is measuring labor, natural resources, time, cash, or inventory, the values for those entities will be expressed in monetary terms.

The Periodicity Principle

Periodicity is an accounting concept that assumes that records of company's financial activities will be organized according to annual, quarterly, and monthly statements. To create accurate financial statements for a company, financial transactions must be identified as belonging to an identifiable financial period.

The Going Concern Principle

This accounting principle assumes that all of the business activity as reflected in the financial transaction recorded in journals and ledgers is for a business entity whose operations can be considered ongoing. In other words, the assumption made when accounting for the business's finances is that it will continue to operate as a business for an indefinite period of time into the future.

The Historical Cost Principle

This principle assumes that purchases transactions recorded in a company's books will retain the values at the time the asset was purchased. For instance, if real estate was purchased at $500,000 in 2010, that the purchase price will be retained even if the purchase price of the same real estate in 2015 is not $750,000.

The Full Disclosure Principle

This principle assumes that a company's financial statements will reveal all information that is necessary to gain an understanding of their financial condition, especially when withholding such data would result in investors forming an understanding that may be detrimental to their actions.

Generally Agree Accounting Principles (GAAP)

The GAAP are 10 principles that form the foundation of established professional accounting practices in the United States. A complete list of these principles appears in Chapter 5 of this book.

Chapter 13: Fraud and Ethics

Figure 11: Free Image

No one likes to be thought of as dishonest or potentially fraudulent in his or her business dealings, so it is often difficult to discuss the subject of fraud and ethics in accounting. Most businesses are run by honest managers and employee honest workers and staff. Regulatory agencies and the GAAP have made the profession of accounting an efficient and reliable way for professionals, investors, government agencies, financial regulators, bankers, and other shareholders to communicate with one another about important ventures and decisions that sometimes impact large segments of the world's populations.

At the same time, we have all witnessed a recent increase in the occurrence of scandals and corruption at the level of financial accounting that has caused tremendous damage throughout the global system of finance, government, and business. Unfortunately, the more skilled and talented a professional accountant becomes at recording and processing business transactions, the greater opportunities there will be for fraud and deception by hiding embezzlement, misappropriation of funds, and other financial crimes behind financial statements that appear to be legitimate. Perhaps the most famous example was the collapse of Enron Corporation and its accounting from Arthur Andersen, LLP after their efforts to lie to the SEC about their revenues, thereby defrauding their shareholders and many innocent civilians out of billions of dollars. Both corporations collapsed and many people were sent to prison.

The issue of ethics and fraud in accounting goes far beyond a philosophical discussion of right and wrong. Well-disciplined, honest accounting accompanied by due diligence is the lifeblood of the world's economy, and people's lives quite literally depend on the ability and willingness of accountants to keep clean books. This chapter discusses many of these concerns specifically, including the causes of fraud, fraud prevention techniques and how to detect fraudulent accounting on your business.

Fraud: Definition and Causes

Fraud is a deliberately deceptive or otherwise dishonest act by an individual, group, or organization that is intended to impose some type of loss on one party to the benefit of the fraudulent party. Fraud involves a form of deception that results in the victim surrendering some type of legal right, usually unknowingly and as a result of deceptive or misleading information.

There are many types of fraud that range from false claims in advertising campaigns, to political fraud involving false political promises in exchange for political favors, to occupational fraud involving improper use of company resources by employees, to tax fraud involving inaccurate financial reporting to avoid paying taxes, to accounting fraud, in which financial statements conceal of distort the financial condition of a company in order to make the look more profitable or more valuable than it actually is to gain leverage in negotiating with lenders, or to lure potential investors, or to hide wrongdoing from financial regulators.

Fraud has become a very serious and very common problem in business, particularly at the level of large, multinational corporations. In 2001. The collapse of the energy corporation Enron and its accounting form, Andersen Accounting made international headlines when top-level company executives were convicted and sent to prison for filing falsified financial statements with the SEC. During the economic collapse of 2008, many of the financial institutions that were instrumental in the founding of the United States were forced to close as a result of dishonest and fraudulent accounting and bookkeeping practices. All of the most serious financial corruption scandals have occurred since 2000.

The tragedy of financial fraud lies beyond the loss of cherished institutions and the value they bring to society. The financial scandals of 2001 and 2008 affected the lives of millions of Americas, and millions of others around the world, most of whom had no direct relations or equitable interest in Enron or any of the major banks that were forced to close their doors permanently. The profession of accountancy provides all professional accountants with the knowledge, skills, ability, and access to information and resources that require diligent and honest attention to ensure success. At the same time, all professional accountants may be in a better position than most to abuse the laws and regulations that govern the global financial system. As a professional accountant, it is not only your responsibility to balance the books before you close them, but also to watch for signs of fraud and report them immediately if you suspect criminal activity.

What You Can Do to Detect and Prevent Fraud in Your Business

Implementing internal audit controls to detect and stop fraudulent activity early is the best solution to accounting fraud. As a professional accountant, you will be licensed and qualified and in a better position than most to determine how to formulate and implement such programs of fraud detection where you work.

Fraud prevention measures may include:
- routine management reviews
- real-time data transaction analysis
- whistleblower programs
- rigorous client and partner vetting
- soft compliance strategies that discourage company cultures that reward bad behavior, such as tipster hotlines and employee interviews that include qualitative feedback

Accounting audits and workplace mechanisms can be extremely helpful in constructing paper trails to locate individual perpetrators after acts of financial corruption have occurred. However, by the time these few individuals are brought to justice, it's often too late to undo the considerable damage they may have already done. Studies have shown that the most important factor influencing the likelihood that accounting fraud will take place at any given company is whether that company supports a culture in which bad behavior is rewarded and good behavior is punished. Accounting tools should most definitely to be used to ensure that financial records are accurate and that financial statements are transparent and in compliance with all regulations regarding disclosure and due diligence. Accounting tool should also be used to conduct frequent and regular audits to detect possible signs of fraud. Where there's smoke, there's fire, and if you detect accounting irregularities that seem disproportionately large or frequent you should take immediate action—as a licensed CPA, the law requires to act in the interest of the GAAP.

But, most importantly, an ounce of prevention is worth a pound of cure, and stopping fraud before it starts the only to keep the books clean. The following organizations and publications may be helpful if you are interested in formulating a fraud prevention effort:

- AICPA Code of Professional Conduct

- The Association of Certified Fraud Officers – ACFE
- The International Ethics Standards Board for Accountants – IESBA
- Cybercrime: An Overview of the Federal Computer Fraud and Abuse Statute and Related Federal Criminal Laws
- SEC Litigation Releases
- The Alphabetical List of the Most Important Accounting Scandals Across 12 Countries and Beyond since about 1980
- Report to the Nation on Occupational Fraud and Abuse - Association of Certified Fraud Examiners (ACFE)
- PricewaterhouseCoopers Global Economic Crime Survey
- The Cost of Malicious Cyber Activity to the U.S. Economy

Chapter 14: Jobs in Accounting

When many people think about Certified Public Accountants and the accounting profession, they often conjure up an image of a boring, clerical office job crunching numbers with a calculator and spreadsheet to make sure the company has enough money to pay the bills. To be sure, maintaining a close watch on the spending and earning habits of the company whose books you keep is a large part of the accounting professions. However, as this book has shown, accounting is one of the oldest and most well-established professional fields. If anything, the need for the services of qualified accountants has only grown more urgent over time. Unlike many areas of business, in which advances in technology have resulted in a steep decline in the quality and quantity of qualified professionals, the need for highly skilled accountants is even greater now.

The field of accounting offers vast opportunities for people of every background, regardless of their interests. Financial services is the most obvious are in which an accounting degree can lead, but there are also accounting professionals employed in government and public service, as well as a wide variety of private sector enterprises ranging from entertainment and sports to law enforcement and healthcare to education and research.

A career in accounting requires a bachelor's degree and some type of licensing certification, especially for those who want to practice as a Certified Public Accountant. Following are lists of job titles available to qualified applicants at many companies and firms, organized by area:

- Government and Nonprofit Accounting:
    - Fund Accountancy
    - Internal Revenue Service Division of Accountancy
- Public Sector Accounting:
    - Cost Estimator
    - Enrolled Agent
    - Forensic Accountant
    - Real Estate Appraiser
    - Tax Accountant
    - Tax Attorney
    - Tax Preparer
- Private Sector Accounting:

- Accounting Clerk
- Accounts Payable/Receivable Clerk
- Accounting Information System Specialist
- Actuarial Accountant/Insurance Accountant
- Bookkeeping Manager
- Budget Analyst
- Capital Accountant
- Comptroller/Financial Controller
- Cost Accountant
- Environmental Accountant/Sustainability Measurement
- Payroll Accountant

- Financial Services Accounting:
  - Business Valuation Specialist
  - Certified Financial Planner
  - Financial Analyst
  - Tax Consultant

Chapter 15: Glossary

Common Terms Used in Bookkeeping and Accounting

Account: An area in a ledger that is reserved for the recording of specific types of business transactions. For example, all expense transactions will be recorded in the Expenses account.

Accounting: The professional practice of posting bookkeeping records into a ledger, balancing accounts, and producing financial statements.

Accounting Cycle: The complete cycle of processing bookkeeping records, from recording transactions in journal to producing financial statements. The accounting cycle has six steps.

Accounting Equation: The basic accounting equation is Assets = Liabilities + Owners' Equity. The accounting equation is used to ensure that records in a double-entry accounting system are balanced.

Accountant: The professional practice of processing and evaluating bookkeeping records. Sometimes used interchangeably with "bookkeeper."

Accounts Payable (A/P): All records that show the amount of money a company owes for goods and services, which it has not yet paid.

Accounts Receivable (A/R): All records that show the amount of money owed to a company for goods and services, which it has not yet received.

Accrual Accounting: An accounting method that recognizes and records income and expenses at the time they are incurred, instead of at the time they are paid.

Assets: All items owned by a company that represent value to the business.

Bad Debts: Unpaid sales invoices for goods and services already sold that the company has written off as an expense.

Balance Sheet: A financial report that provides information about a company's value. The balance sheet shows the value of a company's assets, liabilities, and equity at a specific point in time. The balance sheet is one of three reports that comprise financial statements. The other two reports are the income statement and the cash flow statement.

Bookkeeper: The professional responsible for recording every daily transaction of a business in a financial journal. Sometimes used interchangeably with "accountant."

Bookkeeping: The practice of recording the details of financial business transactions in a journal.

Budget: A detailed financial plan for future business activities.

Capital: Funds or other forms of fixed assets that have been invested into a business to enable operations.

Cash Accounting: An accounting method that recognizes and records income and expenses at the time they are paid, instead of at the time they are earned or incurred.

Cash Flow: The record of how the money generated by a business is managed. Cash flow statements show how the business owners spend the money generated by operating and non-operating activities.

Chart of Accounts: A list of all the financial accounts contained in a company's general ledger. All accounts belong to one of five main categories: Assets, Liabilities, Equity, Revenue, Cost of Goods Sold, and Expenses. Each individual category contains several accounts to record specific types of transactions.

Closing Balance: The final balance of a ledger account at the end of a business day or bookkeeping or accounting cycle.

Coding: The practice of classifying transactions according to the chart of accounts.

Contra: A type of ledger account that allows accountants to counterbalance entries. For example, the Allowance for Bad Debts account is a contra account that allows accountants to resolve discrepancies in the Sales Revenue account.

Cost of Goods Sold: The money spent by a company to purchase inventory items for retail sales. This value can also refer to the cost of raw materials purchased for the manufacture of products for resale.

Credit: Accounting entries that occupy the right side of a double-entry ledger. Credits increase the value of income, liability, and equity accounts and decrease the value of asset and expense accounts.

Credit Note: A transaction record issued when money is refunded to a customer.

Creditor: Anyone who lends money or extends credit.

Data: All of the information recorded in journals and ledgers.

Debit: Accounting entries that occupy the left side of a double-entry ledger. Debits decrease the value of income, liability, and equity accounts and increase the value of asset and expense accounts.

Debtor: Anyone who borrows money.

Deductible: Any business purchase that can be recorded in the business's expense account.

Depreciation: The practice of recording the cost of purchasing fixed assets over their entire useful life.

Double-Entry: Double-entry accounting requires two entries for every transaction—a debit entry and a credit entry. Accountants must ensure that the value of all debit entries equals the value of all credit entries for every accounting cycle.

205

Drawing: An account that records payment of the owner's salary.

Entry/Entries: A single transaction recorded in a company's ledger.

Equity: The amount of financial interest the owner and/or shareholders have in a business. Equity is the difference between the value of assets and liabilities.

Expense: Any business purchases that support operations.

Financial Statements: Specific types of financial reports that show investors, managers, and regulators the financial health of a company. The three types of financial statements are the balance sheet, income statement, and the cash flow statement.

Fiscal Year: A period spanning 12 consecutive months and that constitutes an entire accounting cycle. A fiscal year can begin in any calendar month.

Gross Profit: The value of a business's income that remains after subtracting the cost of goods sold.

Income: All of the money earned by a business, either through the sales of goods and services, or through interest earned and investments.

Inventory: Items owned by a company that are available for sale.

Invoice: A document that provides the details of purchases, such as the goods or services purchased, the purchase date, and the purchase amount.

Journal: A chronological record of daily business transactions maintained by a bookkeeper. Also known as the book of original entry.

Ledger: The volume to which journal transactions are posted by the accountant; the permanent record of daily business transactions, organized by account type.

Liability: All of the money that a company owes.

Loan: Money given to a company or person on the condition that it will be repaid according to specified terms, usually with interest.

Loss: A financial result that occurs when expenses are greater than income. The opposite of profit.

Net Profit: The value of all money earned by a company from operating and non-operating activities, calculated by subtracting the cost of expenses from gross profit.

Opening Balance: The balance of a ledger account on the first day of a financial period.

Payable: A type of expense account that records the amount of money due to be paid by a business.

Payroll: The financial account that records all transactions related to employee wages.

Petty Cash: A financial account that records transactions for minor purchases.

Profit: A financial result that occurs when income is greater than expenses. The opposite of loss.

Purchase: The buying of goods, services, or assets.

Quote: An official estimate of the amount of the cost of goods or services.

Receipt: A document issued to a customer after a purchase that shows the details of the sale.

Receivable: A type of asset account that records the amount of money due to be paid to a business.

Reconcile: The accounting practice of matching balances from one document to another.

Recurring: Any transaction that takes place on a regular, repeating basis, such as a monthly utility bill.

Refund: Money that returned to customers as a result of a dispute, an overpayment, or some other reason.

Reimburse: A payment made to compensate for some type of loss.

Salary: A fixed, predetermined sum of money paid by an employer for an agreed period in exchange for work.

Sales: All money received as a result of goods or services purchased by customers.

Single-Entry: A method of recording transactions in which the transactions are only listed once.

Software: Any type of computer program. Accounting software includes QuickBooks, which automates many accounting tasks.

Statement: A financial report that displays information, such as a bank statement.

Transaction: Any type of business activity that requires a transfer of funds.

Transfer: The movement of monetary funds from one account to another account.

Undeposited Funds: An asset account that shows the amount of money that a company has received but has not yet been deposited into the bank.

Withdrawal: A transaction in which money is taken out of a financial account.

Write-Off: An accounting transaction that officially recognizes that a specified amount of money that is due to be paid will not be received.

Year-End: The period of financial accounting activity that occur at the end of a fiscal year.

Resources

10 Basic Accounting Principles & Key Assumptions - [2019 GAAP Guide]. (n.d.). Retrieved from https://www.myaccountingcourse.com/accounting-principles.

10 Best Jobs for Accounting Majors in 2019. (n.d.). Retrieved from https://www.zippia.com/accounting-major/.

40 Top Paying Accounting Jobs. (2019, September 27). Retrieved from https://www.accounting-degree.org/top-paying-accounting-jobs/.

About the Division of Corporation Finance. (2015, October 5). Retrieved from https://www.sec.gov/divisions/corpfin/cfabout.shtml.

About the Division of Enforcement. (2007, August 2). Retrieved from https://www.sec.gov/enforce/Article/enforce-about.html.

Accessing the U.S. Capital Markets - A Brief Overview for Foreign Private Issuers. (2013, February 20). Retrieved from https://www.sec.gov/divisions/corpfin/internatl/foreign-private-issuers-overview.shtml#IIIB1d2.

Accounting Basics - Income Statement: AccountingCoach. (n.d.). Retrieved from https://www.accountingcoach.com/accounting-basics/explanation/2.

Accounting Basics: Explanation: AccountingCoach. (n.d.). Retrieved from https://www.accountingcoach.com/accounting-basics/explanation.

Accounting Careers. (n.d.). Retrieved from http://www.allaccountingcareers.com/accounting-careers.

Accounting for Inventory and Cost of Goods Sold (COGS): IAS 2 / ASC 330. (n.d.). Retrieved from http://tfageeks.com/accounting-for-inventory-and-cost-of-goods-sold-cogs-ias2-asc360/.

Accounting Jobs. (n.d.). Retrieved from
https://www.glassdoor.com/Job/accounting-jobs-SRCH_KO0,10.htm.

Accounting Principles: Explanation: AccountingCoach. (n.d.). Retrieved from
https://www.accountingcoach.com/accounting-principles/explanation.

AICPA Mission and History. (n.d.). Retrieved from
https://www.aicpa.org/about/missionandhistory.html.

Amortization of Certain Intangible Assets. (2004, December 1). Retrieved from
https://www.journalofaccountancy.com/issues/2004/dec/amortizationofcertainintangibleassets.html.

Amortization of Intangible Assets Definition and Meaning: AccountingCoach. (n.d.). Retrieved from
https://www.accountingcoach.com/terms/A/amortization-of-intangible-assets.

Balance Sheet - Definition & Examples (Assets = Liabilities Equity). (n.d.). Retrieved from
https://corporatefinanceinstitute.com/resources/knowledge/accounting/balance-sheet/.

Balance Sheet Liabilities: AccountingCoach. (n.d.). Retrieved from https://www.accountingcoach.com/balance-sheet/explanation/2.

Balance Sheets, Explained (With Examples): Bench Accounting. (n.d.). Retrieved from https://bench.co/blog/accounting/balance-sheet/.

Basic Accounting Principles - AccountingVerse. (n.d.). Retrieved from https://www.accountingverse.com/accounting-basics/basic-accounting-principles.html.

Basic Cash Flow Statement. (n.d.). Retrieved from https://www.khanacademy.org/economics-finance-domain/core-finance/accounting-and-financial-stateme/financial-statements-tutorial/v/basic-cash-flow-statement.

Bluest, K. (2017, November 21). Bookkeeping: Classification of Accounts. Retrieved from https://smallbusiness.chron.com/bookkeeping-classification-accounts-55421.html.

Blystone, D. (2019, September 17). Understanding Periodic Inventory vs. Perpetual Inventory. Retrieved from https://www.investopedia.com/articles/investing/053115/understanding-periodic-vs-perpetual-inventory.asp.

Bookkeeping - Balance Sheet and Income Statement are Linked: AccountingCoach. (n.d.). Retrieved from https://www.accountingcoach.com/bookkeeping/explanation/11.

Bookkeeping Terms and Basic Accounting Definitions. (n.d.). Retrieved from https://www.beginner-bookkeeping.com/bookkeeping-terms.html.

Bragg, S. (2019, September 16). The periodicity assumption. Retrieved from https://www.accountingtools.com/articles/the-periodicity-assumption.html.

Bragg, S. (2019, January 26). The difference between the periodic and perpetual inventory systems. Retrieved from https://www.accountingtools.com/articles/what-is-the-difference-between-the-periodic-and-perpetual-in.html.

Bragg, S. (2018, December 17). Trial balance: Example: Format. Retrieved from https://www.accountingtools.com/articles/2017/5/16/the-trial-balance-example-format.

Bragg, S. (2018, December 9). Balance sheet. Retrieved from https://www.accountingtools.com/articles/2017/5/11/balance-sheet.

Bragg, S. (2018, May 23). The balance sheet. Retrieved from https://www.accountingtools.com/articles/2017/5/17/the-balance-sheet.

Bragg, S. (2018, July 2). The monetary unit principle. Retrieved from https://www.accountingtools.com/articles/2017/5/15/the-monetary-unit-principle.

Bragg, S. (2018, December 27). Cost of goods sold journal entry. Retrieved from https://www.accountingtools.com/articles/2017/5/13/cost-of-goods-sold-journal-entry.

Bragg, S. (2019, January 12). The income statement. Retrieved from https://www.accountingtools.com/articles/2017/5/17/the-income-statement.

Bragg, S. (2019, August 6). What is GAAP? Retrieved from https://www.accountingtools.com/articles/what-is-gaap.html.

Bragg, S. (2019, August 1). Double entry accounting. Retrieved from https://www.accountingtools.com/articles/2017/5/17/double-entry-accounting.

Bragg, S. (2019, January 21). Cash basis vs. accrual basis accounting. Retrieved from https://www.accountingtools.com/articles/cash-basis-vs-accrual-basis-accounting.html.

Bragg, S. (2019, January 11). Accumulated depreciation. Retrieved from https://www.accountingtools.com/articles/what-is-accumulated-depreciation.html.

Bragg, S. (2019, March 29). Overview of depreciation: Depreciation accounting. Retrieved from https://www.accountingtools.com/articles/2017/5/15/overview-of-depreciation-depreciation-accounting.

Bragg, S. (2019, May 9). Accounting for intangible assets. Retrieved from https://www.accountingtools.com/articles/2017/5/17/intangible-assets-accounting-amortization.

Bragg, S. (2019, August 6). Budget definition. Retrieved from https://www.accountingtools.com/articles/what-is-a-budget.html.

Business Fraud: Culture Is the Culprit. (2017, November 14). Retrieved from https://business-ethics.com/2014/09/23/1840-business-fraud-culture-is-the-culprit/.

Calculating Cost of Goods Sold and Inventory Cost. (n.d.). Retrieved from https://www.dummies.com/business/accounting/calculating-cost-of-goods-sold-and-inventory-cost/.

California, S. of. (n.d.). Retrieved from
http://www.dof.ca.gov/budget/resources_for_departments/budget_analyst_guide/budgeting_accounting_relationship.html.

Careers in Accounting. (n.d.). Retrieved from
https://www.accountingedu.org/career-resources.html.

Cash Basis Accounting vs. Accrual Accounting: Bench Accounting. (n.d.). Retrieved from
https://bench.co/blog/accounting/cash-vs-accrual-accounting/.

Cash Flow Statement. (2019, October 17). Retrieved from
https://en.wikipedia.org/wiki/Cash_flow_statement.

Cash Flow Statement: Explanation: AccountingCoach. (n.d.). Retrieved from
https://www.accountingcoach.com/cash-flow-statement/explanation.

Cash Flow Statements, Explained: Bench Accounting. (n.d.). Retrieved from
https://bench.co/blog/accounting/cash-flow-statements/.

Cash vs Accrual Accounting Explained. (n.d.). Retrieved from https://www.xero.com/us/resources/small-business-guides/accounting/cash-vs-accrual-accounting/.

Chatterjee, A. (n.d.). Top 13 accounting concepts – Explained! Retrieved from https://www.linkedin.com/pulse/top-13-accounting-concepts-explained-aroop-chatterjee.

Chen, J. (2019, October 8). Income statement definition. Retrieved from https://www.investopedia.com/terms/i/incomestatement.asp.

Cost Accounting - Budgeting Analysis. (n.d.). Retrieved from https://www.tutorialspoint.com/accounting_basics/cost_accounting_budgeting_analysis.htm.

Cottonhead, Tessy, Sheoran, M., Wilson, Rajesh, Michelle, ... Sanjana. (2019, September 24). Classification of Accounts - Definition, Explanation and Examples. Retrieved from https://www.accountingformanagement.org/classification-of-accounts/.

Double-entry Bookkeeping System. (2019, October 15). Retrieved from https://en.wikipedia.org/wiki/Double-entry_bookkeeping_system.

Doyle, A. (2019, September 14). Accounting careers: Job options, titles, and descriptions. Retrieved from https://www.thebalancecareers.com/accounting-job-titles-2061488.

Edunote.info@gmail.com. (2019, June 16). 4 accounting assumptions are explained. Retrieved from https://iedunote.com/accounting-assumptions.

Elmblad, S. (2019, May 19). What is double entry accounting? Retrieved from https://www.thebalance.com/what-is-double-entry-accounting-1293675.

Estimated Useful Life and Depreciation of Assets. (2019, September 5). Retrieved from https://www.assetworks.com/useful-life-and-depreciation/.

Ethics and Fraud. (n.d.). Retrieved from https://www.uccs.edu/business/resources/ethics/focus-areas/fraud.

FAF, Financial Accounting Foundation. (n.d.). Retrieved from https://www.accountingfoundation.org/jsp/Foundation/Page/FAFBridgePage&cid=1176164538898.

FASB Accounting Standards Codification®. (n.d.). Retrieved from https://asc.fasb.org/.

FASB, Financial Accounting Standards Board. (n.d.). Retrieved from https://www.fasb.org/jsp/FASB/Page/LandingPage&cid=1175805317350.

Financial Accounting. (n.d.). Retrieved from https://courses.lumenlearning.com/sac-finaccounting/chapter/inventory-methods-for-ending-inventory-and-cost-of-goods-sold/.

Fixed Asset Depreciation: RedBeam Articles. (n.d.). Retrieved from http://www.redbeam.com/fixed-asset-depreciation/.

Freedman, J. (2019, January 28). What is an "ethical issue" in financial accounting? Retrieved from https://smallbusiness.chron.com/ethical-issue-financial-accounting-57889.html.

GASB, Financial Accounting Standards Board. (n.d.). Retrieved from https://www.gasb.org/jsp/GASB/Page/GASBSectionPage&cid=1176168081485.

Generally Accepted Accounting Principles. (n.d.). Retrieved from https://www.cliffsnotes.com/study-guides/accounting/accounting-principles-i/principles-of-accounting/generally-accepted-accounting-principles.

Generally Accepted Accounting Principles (GAAP). (n.d.). Retrieved from https://www.investor.gov/additional-resources/general-resources/glossary/generally-accepted-accounting-principles-gaap.

Generally Accepted Accounting Principles (United States). (2019, October 9). Retrieved from https://en.wikipedia.org/wiki/Generally_Accepted_Accounting_Principles_(United_States).

Grigg, B. A. (2019, October 12). Accounting principles: Definitions and explanations. Retrieved from https://www.fundera.com/blog/accounting-principles.

Hayes, A. (2019, October 8). Balance sheet definition. Retrieved from https://www.investopedia.com/terms/b/balancesheet.asp.

Hayes, A. (2019, October 17). How double entry works. Retrieved from https://www.investopedia.com/terms/d/double-entry.asp.

Hayes, A. (2019, October 16). Understanding cost of goods sold – COGS. Retrieved from https://www.investopedia.com/terms/c/cogs.asp.

Income statement. (2019, September 25). Retrieved from https://en.wikipedia.org/wiki/Income_statement.

Income Statement - Definition, Explanation and Examples. (n.d.). Retrieved from https://corporatefinanceinstitute.com/resources/knowledge/accounting/income-statement/.

Income Statement - Expense and Losses: AccountingCoach. (n.d.). Retrieved from https://www.accountingcoach.com/income-statement/explanation/3.

Income Statements: A Simple Guide: Bench Accounting. (n.d.). Retrieved from https://bench.co/blog/accounting/income-statement/.

Inventory and Cost of Goods Sold: Explanation: AccountingCoach. (n.d.). Retrieved from https://www.accountingcoach.com/inventory-and-cost-of-goods-sold/explanation.

Investopedia. (2019, September 13). The difference between a general ledger and a general journal. Retrieved from https://www.investopedia.com/ask/answers/030915/whats-difference-between-general-ledger-and-general-journal.asp.

Kagan, J. (2019, October 8). Accountant. Retrieved from https://www.investopedia.com/terms/a/accountant.asp.

Katre, H., ProfitBooks, & ProfitBooks. (2018, July 9). What is depreciation - Types, formula & calculation methods for small businesses accounting. Retrieved from https://www.profitbooks.net/what-is-depreciation/.

Kenton, W. (2019, August 22). Trial balance. Retrieved from https://www.investopedia.com/terms/t/trial_balance.asp.

Kenton, W. (2019, October 11). Generally accepted accounting principles (GAAP). Retrieved from https://www.investopedia.com/terms/g/gaap.asp.

Kenton, W. (2019, September 11). Going Concern. Retrieved from https://www.investopedia.com/terms/g/goingconcern.asp.

Kenton, W. (2019, August 28). Salvage value definition. Retrieved from https://www.investopedia.com/terms/s/salvagevalue.asp.

King, S. (n.d.). Cash basis or accrual basis accounting: What's better? Retrieved from https://www.growthforce.com/blog/cash-basis-vs-accrual-basis-accounting-small-medium-businesses.

Ledger, General Ledger Role in Accounting Defined and Explained. (2019, September 11). Retrieved from https://www.business-case-analysis.com/ledger.html#journal242.

Lewis, M. R. (2019, March 29). How to calculate depreciation on fixed assets. Retrieved from https://www.wikihow.com/Calculate-Depreciation-on-Fixed-Assets.

Lewis, M. R. (2019, March 28). How to amortize assets. Retrieved from https://www.wikihow.com/Amortize-Assets.

Li, A. (2016, October 26). The effects of poor ethics in accounting. Retrieved from https://smallbusiness.chron.com/effects-poor-ethics-accounting-37750.html.

Luca Pacioli. (2019, October 21). Retrieved from https://en.wikipedia.org/wiki/Luca_Pacioli.

Manager. (n.d.). Retrieved from https://www.manager.io/guides/9119.

Managerial Accounting. (n.d.). Retrieved from https://courses.lumenlearning.com/sac-managacct/chapter/introduction-to-budgeting-and-budgeting-processes/.

Marendra, D., Fadiyah, S., & Kanya. (2019, March 26). Fixed assets & depreciation: Accounting principles: HashMicro. Retrieved from https://www.hashmicro.com/blog/fixed-assets-depreciation/.

Morah, C. (2019, September 18). How does accrual accounting differ from cash basis accounting? Retrieved from https://www.investopedia.com/ask/answers/09/accrual-accounting.asp.

Murphy, C. B. (2019, June 11). Understanding the cash flow statement. Retrieved from https://www.investopedia.com/investing/what-is-a-cash-flow-statement/.

Murray, J. (2019, January 14). How to amortize intangible assets under IRS section 197. Retrieved from https://www.thebalancesmb.com/amortizing-intangible-assets-under-irs-section-197-398307.

Murray, J. (2019, June 25). Calculating cost of goods sold - Step by step. Retrieved from https://www.thebalancesmb.com/how-to-calculate-cost-of-goods-sold-397501.

Non-GAAP Financial Measures. (2018). Retrieved from https://www.sec.gov/divisions/corpfin/guidance/nongaapinterp.htm.

Northard, A. (2018, September 21). How to depreciate a fixed asset. Retrieved from https://amynorthardcpa.com/how-to-depreciate-a-fixed-asset/.

Periodicity Assumption: Examples. (n.d.). Retrieved from https://www.myaccountingcourse.com/accounting-principles/periodicity-assumption.

Putra, D. (2014, February 2). Basic accounting: Assumptions, principles, constraints. Retrieved from http://accounting-financial-tax.com/2009/08/basic-accounting-assumptions-principles-constraints/.

QuickBooks. (2019, May 9). Cash vs. accrual accounting: What's best for your small business? Retrieved from https://quickbooks.intuit.com/r/bookkeeping/cash-vs-accrual-accounting-whats-best-small-business/.

QuickBooks Canada Team. (2019, March 21). Classifying Assets on Balance Sheet. Retrieved from https://quickbooks.intuit.com/ca/resources/bookkeeping/classifying-assets-balance-sheet/.

Ramsey Solutions. (2019, October 3). What is an accountant and what do they do? Retrieved from https://www.daveramsey.com/blog/what-is-an-accountant.

Research Guides: Accounting: Ethics & fraud. (n.d.). Retrieved from https://guides.emich.edu/accounting/fraud.

Robert Half. (2018, July 26). In-demand accounting jobs - And how to land one. Retrieved from https://www.roberthalf.com/blog/job-market/in-demand-accounting-jobs-and-how-to-land-one.

Ruesink, M. (2018, March 26). 30 basic accounting terms, acronyms and abbreviations students should know. Retrieved from https://www.rasmussen.edu/degrees/business/blog/basic-accounting-terms-acronyms-and-abbreviations-students-should/.

Rules and Regulations for the Securities and Exchange Commission and Major Securities Laws. (2017, May 12). Retrieved from https://www.sec.gov/about/laws/secrulesregs.htm.

Shpak, S. (2019, January 28). Five types of budgets in managerial accounting. Retrieved from https://smallbusiness.chron.com/five-types-budgets-managerial-accounting-50928.html.

Staff, M. F. (2016, February 29). How to calculate the amortization of intangible assets. Retrieved from https://www.fool.com/knowledge-center/how-to-calculate-the-amortization-of-intangible-as.aspx.

Standards & Guidance. (2019, September 27). Retrieved from https://fasab.gov/accounting-standards/.

Statement of Cash Flows - How to Prepare Cash Flow Statements. (n.d.). Retrieved from https://corporatefinanceinstitute.com/resources/knowledge/accounting/statement-of-cash-flows/.

Stimpson, J., Padar, J., Hood, D., Mendlowitz, E., Cohn, M., Lee, D., ... Root, D. (2019, October 21). By Jeff Stimpson. Retrieved from https://www.accountingtoday.com/.

Summary: Budgeting. (n.d.). Retrieved from https://www.accountingtools.com/summary-budgeting.

The 10 Worst Corporate Accounting Scandals of All Time. (2019, August 19). Retrieved from https://www.accounting-degree.org/scandals/.

Top 5 Accounting Jobs. (n.d.). Retrieved from https://www.topaccountingdegrees.org/top-5-accounting-jobs/.

Trial Balance Period in Accounting Cycle Explained with Examples. (2019, September 11). Retrieved from https://www.business-case-analysis.com/trial-balance.html.

Tuovila, A. (2019, September 28). Depreciation. Retrieved from https://www.investopedia.com/terms/d/depreciation.asp.

Tuovila, A. (2019, August 28). Historical Cost Definition. Retrieved from https://www.investopedia.com/terms/h/historical-cost.asp.

Tuovila, A. (2019, May 22). Amortization of intangibles definition. Retrieved from https://www.investopedia.com/terms/a/amortization-of-intangibles.asp.

Tutorials, K. S. (n.d.). Accounting: The income statement and balance sheet. Retrieved from https://www.keynotesupport.com/accounting/accounting-balance-sheet-income-statement.shtml.

Types of Budgets - The Four Most Common Budgeting Methods. (n.d.). Retrieved from https://corporatefinanceinstitute.com/resources/knowledge/accounting/types-of-budgets-budgeting-methods/.

Understanding the Cash Flow Statement. (n.d.). Retrieved from https://www.abc-amega.com/Articles/Credit-Management/understanding-the-cash-flow-statement.

Vaidya, D., Vaidya, D., Vaidya, D., JPMorgan Equity Analyst, & JPMorgan Equity Analyst. (2019, July 22). Cash accounting vs accrual accounting: Top 9 differences. Retrieved from https://www.wallstreetmojo.com/cash-accounting-vs-accrual-accounting/.

Vaidya, D., Vaidya, D., & Vaidya, D. (2019, October 15). Amortization of intangible assets: Examples: Calculate. Retrieved from https://www.wallstreetmojo.com/amortization-of-intangible-assets/.

Ward, S. (2019, June 11). What exactly is a balance sheet? Retrieved from https://www.thebalancesmb.com/balance-sheet-definition-2946947.

What are the accounting principles, assumptions, and concepts?: AccountingCoach. (n.d.). Retrieved from https://www.accountingcoach.com/blog/accounting-principles-assumptions.

What Is A Balance Sheet: AccountingCoach. (n.d.). Retrieved from https://www.accountingcoach.com/balance-sheet/explanation.

What Is a Budget?: AccountingCoach. (n.d.). Retrieved from https://www.accountingcoach.com/blog/what-is-a-budget-2.

What Is a Trial Balance?: AccountingCoach. (n.d.). Retrieved from https://www.accountingcoach.com/blog/what-is-a-trial-balance.

What Is Accounting, Exactly?: Bench Accounting. (n.d.). Retrieved from https://bench.co/blog/accounting/what-is-accounting/.

What Is Accounting? (2019, August 19). Retrieved from https://www.accounting-degree.org/what-is-accounting/.

What Is Budgeting?: AccountingCoach. (n.d.). Retrieved from https://www.accountingcoach.com/blog/what-is-budgeting.

What Is Periodicity in Accounting?: AccountingCoach. (n.d.). Retrieved from https://www.accountingcoach.com/blog/what-is-periodicity-in-accounting.

What Is the Difference between Inventory and the Cost of Goods Sold?: AccountingCoach. (n.d.). Retrieved from https://www.accountingcoach.com/blog/what-is-the-difference-between-inventory-and-the-cost-of-goods-sold.

What Is the Difference between the Cash Basis and the Accrual Basis of Accounting?: AccountingCoach. (n.d.). Retrieved from https://www.accountingcoach.com/blog/cash-basis-accrual-basis-of-accounting.

What Is the Double-entry System?: AccountingCoach. (n.d.). Retrieved from https://www.accountingcoach.com/blog/what-is-the-double-entry-system.

What Is the Income Statement?: AccountingCoach. (n.d.). Retrieved from https://www.accountingcoach.com/blog/what-is-the-income-statement.

Wood, M. (2019, August 3). Cash flow statement: What it is, example, and how to prepare one. Retrieved from https://www.fundera.com/blog/cash-flow-statement.

Writers, S. (2019, October 21). Career, degree and job information. Retrieved from https://www.accounting.com/.

Writers, S. (2019, July 22). The comprehensive guide to understanding GAAP. Retrieved from https://www.accounting.com/resources/gaap/.

ZipRecruiter. (n.d.). Retrieved from https://www.ziprecruiter.com/g/10-Most-Popular-Types-of-Accounting-Jobs.

CPSIA information can be obtained
at www.ICGtesting.com
Printed in the USA
JSHW011953130420
5046JS00015B/1371